The Awakening Conscience, by William Holman Hunt, R.A.
From the painting in the possession of Sir Colin Anderson.

MARY PETER

Collecting Victoriana

Drawings in the Text

by

JENEFER PETER

FREDERICK A. PRAEGER, Publishers

New York · Washington

BOOKS THAT MATTER

PUBLISHED IN
THE UNITED STATES OF AMERICA IN 1968
BY FREDERICK A. PRAEGER, INC., PUBLISHERS
111 FOURTH AVENUE, NEW YORK, N.Y. 10003
SECOND PRINTING, 1969

LIBRARY OF CONGRESS CATALOG CARD NUMBER:
68-23167

PRINTED IN GREAT BRITAIN

To L. W. and L. K., and
to Keith who nagged

ACKNOWLEDGEMENTS

I WOULD particularly like to thank the following: Mr Kenneth Hendry, Mr James Manning, Mr Brian Chase, Miss Jenefer Peter, Miss Enid Phillips, Miss Daphne Christopherson, and Mr and Mrs James Barber for help with the manuscript and illustrations; and Mrs M. M. Spear, Mrs O. E. Johnson, Mrs May, Miss Childs, the Misses M. and D. Jolly, Mrs Philip Williams, Mr John Liddiat and Mr Keith Loze for their kindness in allowing the use of materials from their collections for illustration.

I am most grateful to Sir Colin Anderson for his kind permission to reproduce *The Awakening Conscience* by William Holman Hunt as a frontispiece to this book, and to Mr A. A. Cumming, Curator of the City Museum and Art Gallery (Plates 2, 4-16, 18-32), the William Morris Gallery, Walthamstow (Plate 3), the Victoria and Albert Museum, London (Figures 24 and 27), and to Miss Elizabeth Aslin (Figure 28) for permission to reproduce the illustrations in the book. I am indebted to Mr Cyril Staal for helpful advice, and to Lady Mander, for it is to her and Miss Griffiths that I owe a tour of Wightwick which was an inspiration.

I acknowledge my indebtedness to the following books dealing with Victoriana: *Nineteenth Century Furniture*, by Elizabeth Aslin; *Nineteenth Century English Glass*, by Hugh Wakefield; *Victorian Porcelain*, by Geoffrey Godden; and finally, Margaret Flower's *Victorian Jewellery*.

CONTENTS

ILLUSTRATIONS

Collecting Victoriana

CHAPTER I

INTRODUCTION

THE VICTORIAN age in its vigour and richness challenges the Elizabethan. An age of expansion, with a growing and prosperous Empire; of great contrasts, with its background of the Industrial Revolution enriching some, raising upper and middle class standards of life, but condemning many to the fate of an industrial proletariat. The growing materialism was balanced by a religious revival, the consequences of which are still working themselves out today. The tenderness, not to say mawkishness, of its domestic ideals was in abject contrast to the proportion of domestic tyrants it produced (Mr Barrett of Wimpole Street is the classic example), and to the raffish dissipation which actually flourished discreetly in the cities. It was a period of great characters and eccentrics, not least of them those who dominated the art and literature of the time. Because of an intense individualism coupled with increasing command of industrial processes, and the added discoveries of archaeology, there was an intense battle of the styles in architecture and the arts. The collector of Victoriana has a vast range to choose from.

Unfortunately, the tremendous vigour and inventiveness of the Victorians very often produced hideous over-elaboration, or copies of past styles which were dead copies and nothing else. Because of this, the very real charm and originality of their things have been in danger of being forgotten. Twentieth century people look with horror and amazement at the immense show-pieces of the Great Exhibition, forgetting the small and seemly pieces which were quietly adorning houses

at the same time. It is for these smaller things that the collector of Victoriana looks today.

The fantastic turreted mansion which was the Victorian
magnate's dream is now unmanageably out of date, and its
vast furniture and fittings are unregretted. Small Victorian
furniture intended for the simpler houses, needlework, china,
glass, and the endearing trinkets which were so beautifully
made, so charming in colour, are the things most sought.
A prolific and prodigal age, the Victorian produced a vast
amount of clutter. Amongst this clutter, we can afford to
select. It is easy to dismiss a photograph of a Victorian
drawing-room, potted palms, occasional tables loaded with
bibelots, what-nots, draped and mirrored overmantel and all,
as a horror. Remove the potted palms, remove draperies and
overmantel, space out the bibelots, and the charm returns.
It is the lavishness, the ill use of good material that is so
offensive. The Victorians had so many charming things, they
were overpowered with their own richness and overloaded
everything. We of course can be grateful for the lavishness,
because the more survives for us. In an age dominated by
mass production, we can take pleasure in the last period of
careful craftsmanship; amongst the intense brilliancy of
modern machine-made dyes, we can rest our eyes gratefully
on the softness and brightness of early Victorian colours.
And if at one end of the period—up to about 1845—we can
rejoice in the sureness of proportion and good cabinet-making
still surviving from the Georgian, at the other we can see
the emergence of the forerunners of the modern movement.
The pedigree of our best craftsmen-designed furniture today
leads back surely to William Morris and Philip Webb, to
Gimson and Voysey, whilst the foundations of the tradition
which has produced the work of the modern artist potters
may be discovered in the unassuming vernacular productions
of the local potteries, such as the Nottingham saltglaze and
North Devon harvest-ware, and in the work of the Martin

brothers, whose finest pots mark them as the forerunners of a new period.

For the purposes of this survey, I have divided the reign into periods—Early, up to the Great Exhibition of 1851; Middle, 1851-1875; and Late, 1875-1901; and as a basis I have considered the furnishings of a middling-sized house, room by room, giving silver, jewellery and trinkets, china and glass, more expanded treatment on their own. It is the contents of these middle class houses which turn up most often in antique and junk shops and sale rooms. As a basis I have taken a sale catalogue for the contents of No. 45 Emma Place, East Stonehouse, which was sold by Messrs Skardon of Plymouth in 1841. This stucco terrace house was furnished just at a time when Victoriana was most charming, light and uncluttered, and from it one can move forward in time, using it as a standard of comparison for later rooms. But I also hope to show that, although the overall effect of later interiors might be ill-assorted and ugly, it is still possible to pick out good things from the general confusion, and that by those with eyes to see, charming pieces may be found belonging to every decade of Victoria's reign.

But the eye must be trained. Museum collections like those of the Victoria and Albert and the London Museums, by-gones and folk museums, and Victorian country houses open to the public will help. Wherever possible, study-collections should be consulted—especially in the case of china and glass, which lose so much of their texture under glass and artificial display lighting, and should ideally be handled for their characteristics to be properly learned. Galleries as well as museums are very useful. A morning looking at the nineteenth century English artists in the Tate Gallery takes one straight back into the Victorian's world. Pre-Raphaelites, *genre* painters like Frank Potter, Martineau and Augustus Egg, Millais and even Watts (especially in his portraits of Victorian worthies), set the scene. Here are not only the perfect period interiors all in colour, but the people who inhabited them, seen with the vision of their own time, its own peculiar romantic sensibility. Entering their world, one gradually learns that indefinable, intuitive thing, a question of flavour and atmosphere; period-sense.

CHAPTER II

THE DINING-ROOM

WHEN the contents of No. 45 Emma Place were sold in 1841, the dining-room and drawing-room and the best bedroom contained the most important lots in the house. The dining-room in its state, supplied with plate, china and glass (sold with the contents of the kitchen and butler's pantry), was its central room, the hub of the family life. Here were the mahogany dining table and chairs, the mahogany brass-bound cellaret, the Broadwood pianoforte. Later in the century, the emphasis was to change subtly. The parlour or drawing-room gained in importance as the chief state rooms in the middle class home. As the standards of middle class life improved, the number of useless possessions acquired purely for display grew. So the Victorian drawing-room's bibelots and trinkets increased. In 1841 things retained a memory of Georgian plainness; furniture and ornaments were in a seemly way, and the random profusion of the sixties and seventies was still to come. Even so, Victorian dining-room furniture of all periods is amongst the easiest to accommodate in modern houses. For the dining-room remained a functional room, dedicated to that very good and substantial thing, the enjoyment of Victorian cooking. The nonsense that invaded the drawing-room was out of place in territory dominated by Mrs Beeton.

The dining-room furniture of 1841 is still easy to acquire, and comparatively cheap, and because of its plainness, neatness of proportion and good craftsmanship, very well worth having. It might be called the poor man's Regency, for the

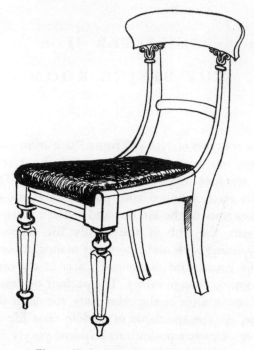

Fig. 1. Early Victorian dining chair.

shapes of chairs and tables follow the same principles, but it is Regency fattened up. Just as the simple princess lines of Regency dresses were replaced by the nipped-in waists, drooping shoulders and heavy puffed sleeves of the eighteen-thirties and forties, so the lines of the furniture were weakened in the same way. The square trim of Regency dining chairs is replaced by a curved back (Fig. 1), classical lines are softened, and the ubiquitous turned leg and stretcher rails make their appearance (see the drawing-room chairs Fig. 14). At Emma Place there were six dining chairs with cane seats and cushions, their wood not noted, but probably mahogany as they accompanied a 'set of Mahogany Telescope Dining Tables with additional Leaves' and the brass-bound cellaret.

Mahogany and rosewood were the timbers most popular—
rosewood a survival from Regency times, the more florid
mahogany gaining ground as time went on. The chiffonier
at Emma Place was listed as 'imitation rosewood', probably
that 'faux bois de Rose'—the Seychelles rosewood—dark
red or claret coloured and smelling of roses when rubbed.
The chiffonier was a low mahogany or rosewood cupboard
of Regency descent used both as a display cabinet for china
and as a cupboard for such things as decanters—at Emma
Place it obviously took the place of a sideboard. As a smaller
and more compact object it is obviously more useful than the
rather over-generous sideboards of early Victorian houses.
Nevertheless, the sideboard of the eighteen-forties is not to
be despised, and given the space to display, these sideboards
have a certain nobility in their weighty plainness. They are
basically the same as Regency in shape, but heavier and
larger in all their parts, their mouldings florid and a trifle
coarse, often classical, sometimes with the acanthus motif,
but still in a vigorous way, immensely pleasing, made of
beautiful timber, often with a fine sense of the figure of the
wood (Fig. 2).

At Emma Place, the Broadwood 'fine toned Pianoforte'
and stool (covered with morocco), and a guitar were kept in
the dining-room. Also a pair of ottomans and a mahogany

Fig. 2. Early Victorian sideboard.

sofa table which showed that the room was used for sitting as well as dining. The *ottomans* would be shaped much as they were in Regency times—low, backless upholstered seats, probably covered with buttoned fabric. Victorian piano stools are examples of the less desirable aspect of Victoriana—more ingenious than graceful, adjustable, often over-padded and lumpish. The small Victorian *sofa table* or occasional table, however, is a most desirable acquisition. Until far into the period these unassuming and small tables kept their neat proportions. Occasionally one finds an example with a clumsy central pedestal, bulbous with over-florid moulding, or too elaborate turning: generally, however, these adornments are no worse than an amusing *gaucherie*. Sofa tables were circular, on a central pedestal often with triangular foot, and might be solid, in mahogany or rosewood (Fig. 3), or later on in walnut, or veneered, with bands of contrasting woods laid in. In the eighteen-fifties or sixties, they might be finished off with a beaded moulding. These useful little tables are increasingly sought after, yet still may be found in junk and antique shops at reasonable prices. Often they may need attention, because of chipped or risen veneer, but this is a job that can be done at home, with a little skill and patience, or dealt with by a local cabinet-maker.

The moderate sized Victorian pedestal dining table is equally desirable. Again, the wood may need attention, but scratched or stained surfaces may usually be put right by sandpapering down, waxing and sandpapering again, until the desired fresh surface is brought up. As a functional piece of furniture, the Victorian circular table did not suffer the elaboration, the unwise experiments in proportion, which disfigured other more decorative pieces of furniture. The central pedestal might be unwieldly, with bulbous moulding, or slightly spoiled in the eighteen fifties with an over-ingenious open-work pedestal; even so the great circular lake of beautifully figured, highly-polished wood was still attractive.

Fig. 3. Early Victorian sofa table (left) and two circular
dining tables.

Country-bred pieces retained a charming simplicity far into
the period. The table illustrated (Fig. 3, centre), beautifully
made in beechwood, was picked up at a local sale for a very
small price. The oval table with its somewhat sea-weedy inlay
and complicated support shows the decline of this essentially
simple and solid shape into over-elaboration which occurred
in the eighteen-sixties (Fig. 3, right).

The dining-room at Emma Place, like other dining-rooms
of the eighteen-forties, still retained something of Regency
lightness. The curtains, of damask moreen, were draped on
a pole, with gilded holders: one may imagine it, white-
painted, reeded, given a touch of grandeur by its gilded
mounting. Leech's illustrations to Surtees give many such
dining-rooms, their colour schemes often white-walled, set off
with red curtains and upholstery, the fine fat gilding of
picture frames or looking-glass over the chimney-piece giving
a rich effect. At Emma Place the chimney-piece ensemble
had its rich glitter provided by a 'Highly Polished Steel Fire

Set' and a 'Bronze Fender'. Its adornment was simple—
'Pair Fire Screens and Hyacinth Glass 1 Foreign China Tea
Pot, Pair ditto Jars, Fish Globe, Print, framed and glazed'.
The 'Foreign China' suggests something of the simplicity
of a Georgian chimney-piece garniture. A few years later its
place might be taken by two tinkling glass lustres, perhaps
in rose red and clear glass, and a central clock, probably under
a glass dome. Fenders and fire-sets have, alas, nearly all disappeared. In their small-metalwork the Victorians, throughout the period, showed their best craftsmanship and the
beauty of simple functional toolmaking. The humble Victorian firetongs or brass-mounted toasting fork are delightful,
neatly proportioned things and well worth searching for.

In their pole-screens also the Victorians produced objects
of great charm, although the florid turning of the mahogany
pole was sometimes rather overwhelming. Frames could be
shield-shaped or rectangular, to be raised or lowered at will,
to keep direct heat off the face, the inner side of the screen
embroidered or decorated with bead-work or ribbon-work.
The true charm of the period becomes apparent in these
lovingly worked bouquets of full-blown roses and other
flowers, in gros point or in cross stitch, with their soft colours
or in bead-work of subtle and tender silvery tones.

Unfortunately, the charm of the eighteen-forties began to
languish all too soon. The influence of the Great Exhibition
of 1851 was unhappy. Ingenuity and fertility of invention
outran disciplined design. Elaboration and novelty for its
own sake came into favour. The invention of aniline dyes
produced colours of a sharpness to set one's teeth on edge—
prussian blue, malachite green, and a strong chrome yellow
were typical of the tones which replaced the old soft shades
which had given early Victorian embroidery and textiles such
charm. These new and savage colours used with discretion
might still be telling but in the hugger-mugger profusion of
the rooms of the eighteen-sixties they shouted for attention.

And the Great Exhibition had let loose a fashion for needless profusion: manufacturers vied with each other to show new shapes and styles of furniture, with every kind of gadget available. A vast choice of bogus antique was brought before the public; a free version of Renaissance, a sort of medieval actually nearer Jacobean in spirit, and an interpretation of French style favouring Louis XIV, Louis XV and Louis XVI or the plushy elaboration of the second Empire. The French styles—which relied upon aggravated curves, serpentine fronts, chairs with curved backs and cabriole legs for their effect— were the most popular, although styles in the general clutter of one room might be hopelessly mixed. Furniture echoed the fashionable crinoline; everything that could be was draped, table-cloths in folds to the ground, even chimney-pieces edged with bobbled fringe, whilst chairs were buttoned, tufted, corded and upholstered with every kind of elaboration. Worst of all the dining-room lost its lightness. The ideal of massive solidity dominated Victorian interiors in the middle period, in which the weighty solemnity of the appointments of hall and dining-room provided what was thought a necessary contrast to the lightness and elegance of the drawing-room. Dining-rooms became deep caves of red flock and damask wallpaper and vast mahogany furniture.

Ever since the eighteen-thirties or earlier, stimulated by Scott's novels and the romantic lithographs of cavalier and roundhead country houses by Joseph Nash, there had been an antiquarian vogue in dining-room furniture. Neo-jacobean furniture of this early period has a certain charm, and the pieces surviving at Cotehele, Cornwall, do not look out of place in their highly romantic setting. But that battle of the styles let loose by the Great Exhibition produced nothing as good. Commercialized and crude, at its best it has a weighty magnificence, a character which can be overpowering—at its worst, with stuck-on machine-made ornament and sticky French-polished mahogany, it is just vulgar. The *side-*

Fig 4. Sideboard. In mahogany and plate glass. Made and
exhibited by Messrs Howard & Son, Great Exhibition 1851.

board gained status and lost its shape. B. J. Talbert, whose
Gothic Forms Applied to Furniture appeared in 1873,
reckoned it the most important piece of furniture in the
dining-room and therefore included many designs for it. The
example illustrated was a design produced for the Great
Exhibition and shows the curves and cresting of the French
style (Fig. 4). Worse was to come, for the sideboard gained
shelves for the display of china and plate, sometimes a
weighty cornice and moulding. Reformers of English taste
such as Sir Charles Lock Eastlake, Director of the National
Gallery, whose *Hints on Household Taste* had a considerable
following amongst the enlightened, and Morris, Faulkner,
Marshall and Company, who embodied William Morris's
ideals, did not help the sideboard at all. Eastlake's designs
were of a painstakingly integrity and square hewn ugliness
(Fig. 5 shows one of them). Morris & Faulkner's sideboards,
despite the nostalgic richness of the painted decoration

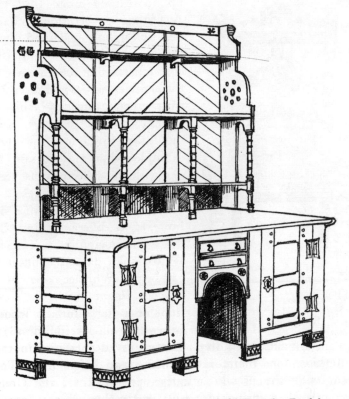

Fig. 5. Sideboard from *Hints on Household Taste* by Eastlake.

and their fine workmanship, have an uncertainness about
their proportions. The reformers' effect was to set for generations the idea of a sideboard as a cupboard with shelves
above, the old generous amplitude and spreading proportions
of a Regency or early Victorian sideboard was gone for ever.

The passion for novelty even affected the shape of dining-
room chairs and table. Oblong, oval and rectangular tables
replaced the old central pedestal round table. Sir Charles
Eastlake provided designs for a gaunt refectory type. Most
odious were heavily baronial suites of table and chairs done

Fig. 6. Dining room chair, c. 1870

up in turkey work (Fig. 6). A fireside or occasional chair, heavily upholstered and buttoned might have a lumpish, cosy charm but on the whole the eighteen-sixties and seventies with their unwieldy shapes, knobbly with turning and moulding, hit a new low. For examples that are pleasant to live with the collector must seek amongst the smaller things.

Late Victorian furniture is, however, a different thing. By the eighteen-eighties a reaction against solid dark magnificence had begun. Whistler's celebrated *Peacock Room* was in the forefront of a vogue for the Japanese, with all its lightness. A new and almost flimsy gaiety invaded dining-rooms. A fashion for Adam, Hepplewhite and Sheraton flooded them with the pseudo-antiques with which Tissot's and Orchardson's paintings are full; pretty, but slightly weedy near-Georgian. This, although it has an unmistakably Victorian air, is still near enough to the original to provide a worthy poor man's Georgian. It is, unless masquerading as eigtheenth-century work, still fairly reasonable.

This revolution in taste was partly social, partly to do with the influence of the artist craftsmen grouped together with Morris and the 'artistic' writers such as Ruskin and Eastlake. Although Morris furniture might be bought by a comparatively small public, its influence was great. Hence the 'aesthetic' households and the 'greenery-yallery' style of the eighties lampooned by Du Maurier in *Punch*, laughed at but gradually accepted. Ruskin and Eastlake had condemned fashion, tried to bring back beauty. Morris showed how this should be done, not in his medievalizing efforts but in his respect for the character of his materials and his rediscovery of the tradition of native furniture making, before the Restoration and the domination of fashion.

Morris showed the way, but Ernest Gimson and Sidney Barnsley brought about a new and truly contemporary style. Both had been trained as architects and were closely familiar with the building trades and Ernest Gimson was himself a very fine executant craftsman. Gimson came to London in 1886 and died in Gloucestershire in 1919. During that time the foundations of modern English furniture design were laid. He rediscovered the natural beauty of wood, using English walnut, oak and yew, often using inlay of bone,

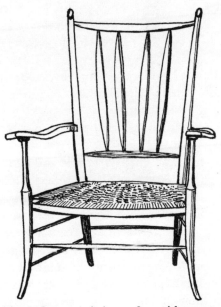

Fig. 7. Low armchair, c. 1890, with woven string seat.

ebony, mother of pearl, cherry or holly on sideboards and chests. Dining chairs were rush seated, with bobbin-turned spindles and ladder backs, including a new type of back with two vertical and three horizontal members within the frame. Gimson's furniture had a new vertical emphasis, a lightness and simplicity of shape. This vertical emphasis was taken further by Voysey—better known as an architect, but a fine designer as well—who humanized the strange vertical shapes of the *art nouveau* movement beginning on the Continent into acceptable English furniture. Gimson and Voysey dining-room chairs and tables are the prototypes of the modern craftsman-built furniture of today. Work by the masters themselves may be difficult to find and costly, but unassuming pieces in the tradition may be picked up. The low chair illustrated (Fig. 7) was bought in a second-hand shop at Newlyn, where the Newlyn school of artists settled in the eighties.

CHAPTER III

THE DRAWING-ROOM

THE VICTORIAN drawing-room of all periods, early, middle or late is the richest field for the collector. On the drawing-room the Victorians lavished their most cherished and often their most charming ideas. It was also the room in which some of their worst nonsense was freely expressed.

The drawing-room of 1841 was the prettiest and least cluttered of Victorian drawing-rooms. At Emma Place it seems to have been a crimson, gold and white room, simply but richly furnished in rosewood. A 'set of splendid Crimson Damask Moreen and Muslin curtains' was accompanied by a matching couch ('with an additional stripe cover') in rosewood and eight drawing-room chairs 'to correspond'. There was also a 'Centre Ottoman covered with Crimson Velvet, handsomely embroidered'. An easy chair covered in crimson moreen also and a Brussels carpet and rug to correspond might seem to have produced rather an overpoweringly red effect, but this was relieved by sumptuous gilding—gilt curtain pole, gold-framed prints on the walls, a 'Brilliant Single Plate Chimney Glass, in Carved and Burnished Gold Frame' —and a certain amount of glittering cut glass.

To begin at the chimney piece. Much was made of the Emma Place glass being a 'Single Plate'; the bland expanse of Victorian plate does not impress us in the same way, rather the opposite. Nevertheless, Victorian chimney mirrors are very worth acquiring. Later ones share in the general decline, are fussy with shelves and compartments and have the

31

character of an overmantel, but early Victorian wall-glass can
be extremely pretty. On the chimney piece itself must have
stood the 'Pair of Ground and Cut Glass Flower Stands' and
the 'Pair of Burnished Gold and Flowered Candlesticks'
perhaps accompanied by the 'Full Length Figure of Mrs
Hannah More under a glass shade'. This extraordinary pre-
dilection for glass shades over almost every kind of ornament
persisted throughout the period—until the eighteen-seventies
at least. Tenniel's Alice climbing through the looking glass
was drawn stepping carefully round a French clock enclosed
in a glass dome. Glass shades were in effect small show-cases
and were beautifully made, lined with velvet and with a
mahogany moulding at the base. Sometimes, the objects put
under the glass were singularly inappropriate: a composition
stone bull, after a famous Renaissance statue; a model of

the Drake Memorial at Tavi-
stock (at Buckland Abbey) and
this figure of Hannah More,
writer and philanthropist. Bouquets of wax, shell or feather
flowers, or even flowers made
of bread, which were all more
or less fragile conceits, might
need the shelter of glass, but
some glass domes were more
fantastic than decorative or
useful.

Flowers made of bread or
wax, beadwork and embroidery
were all polite crafts practised
by early Victorian ladies. They
were symptoms of a new leisure,
just as the elaborate occasional
furniture with which drawing-

Fig. 8. Early Victorian tea poy.   rooms began to fill were signs

Hand fire-screens in papier-mâché with painted landscapes and a figure subject in oils: *c.* 1845. (*City Art Gallery, Plymouth*).

Drawing-room screen designed by A. H. Mackmurdo. (*William Morris Gallery, Walthamstow*).

Copper pudding and jelly moulds: mid-nineteenth century. (*Buckland Abbey*).
Copper mould for a cream: mid-nineteenth century. (*Buckland Abbey*).

of a rising standard of life. In 1841 the middle class
drawing-room of Emma Place was relatively simple. Even
so, Emma Place boasted a 'Looe (*sic*) Table on Pedestal
and Block' and a 'Pair of Card ditto to correspond'. From
the forties onwards there was a proliferation of occasional
tables, for every purpose. Our illustration shows a *Tea Poy*
(Fig. 8), in effect a tea-caddy mounted on a table. Very similar
was the *work table*, in which sewing materials could be kept.
This was often lined with silk. The *games table* shown with
its marquetry inlay was probably made about 1850 (Fig. 9).
Its top would fold flat, so that it could stand upright like a
screen. The card tables at Emma Place were probably of a
folding rectangular type, likewise to be stood when idle as a
sort of side table against a wall (Fig. 10).

Fig. 9. Games table, with marquetry inlay, c. 1850.

C

Fig. 10. Early Victorian card table in rosewood, c. 1840.

Fig. 11. Upholstered sociable, c. 1850.

The central *ottoman* with its embroidery, plushily covered
in crimson velvet, would be a far more elaborate piece than
the ottomans of the dining-room. Dicky Doyle did a drawing
of its final stage of development—his *After Dinner* of 1864,
where ladies in enormous crinolines are seated all around a
vast ottoman and the billowing curves of crinoline and upholstery together have a certain hippopotamus charm. The
specimen of 1841 would be lighter, less voluminous. These
extraordinary cross-bred pieces of furniture, the serpentine
seat and the *sociable* (Fig. 11), had not yet appeared. Such
variations between ottoman, chair and sofa were developed
in the fifties and sixties. The *sofa* of 1841 had not quite lost
the grace of its Regency beginnings: the famous picture by
David of Madame Recamier shows its original lightness and
delicacy; by 1841 it had become cobbier, more sturdy in all
its parts, but it is a type of furniture which throughout the
period never completely lost its charm. The original Regency
specimens had been painted or inlaid, made in woods such
as beech; the lighter woods were now replaced by the ubiquitous mahogany or rosewood. The stuffed bolster cushions persisted as a fitting throughout all phases—though when hard
stuffed and covered in black horse-hair late in the period,
sofa and cushions looked intimidating rather than comfort-

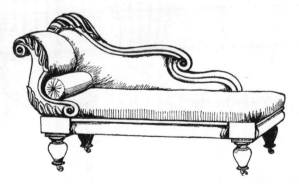

Fig. 12. Sofa, with horsehair upholstery, c. 1845.

Fig. 13. Sofa upholstered in horsehair, c. 1851.

able. In the forties, however, covered with velvet or with the damask moreen or striped covers used at Emma Place, they were delightful. R. B. Martineau's picture at Birmingham Art Gallery, *The Last Chapter*, shows the early Victorian sofa at its best; lit by the firelight it looks enticingly comfortable in its striped silk covers; its bolster-cushion with neatly pleated and buttoned ends. Fig. 12 shows an early version of the sofa, and Fig. 13 a model of 1851.

The Victorian drawing-room housed a great variety of chairs. First the drawing-room chair proper. In 1841 these

Fig. 14. Early Victorian drawing-room chairs.

were still of Regency type, their design subtly softened as if they echoed the changed shapes of fashionable clothes. (Fig. 14, A, B and C). These were made in mahogany or rosewood with turned legs and stretchers, with seats of horsehair, damask or velvet, often decorated with an embroidered flower bouquet. In the drawing-rooms of great houses they might be gilded. Fig. 14, C shows one from a Cornish country house. In 1841 there was already a fair number of types of occasional chair, though the variety had greatly increased by the fifties and sixties. Emma Place boasted an 'Imitation Rosewood Easy Chair, Covered Crimson Moreen'. This was probably of *bergère* shape with upholstered back and arm rests and cabriole legs (Fig. 15). Already, by this time there were the *Abbotsford* type of chair—so called after Scott's novel which had inspired its pseudo-ancient proportions—and the *prie-dieu* with the top of its long back turned into an arm rest for prayer.

Chairs with long backs such as these were ideal backgrounds for needle-work panels—most often carried out in Berlin wool-

Fig. 15. Easy chair (bergère shape), c. 1840.

work, like the panel on the chair in F. G. Stephen's picture
Mother and Child at the Tate Gallery. Although the heaviness of moulding and unwieldy arms may mean the chair
is itself slightly later in date (c. 1850). Berlin work was so
called because in 1810 a Berliner had some designs printed
for his wife to work embroidery from and then started to
sell the prints. These were drawn out on squared paper, hand-
coloured with every square representing a stitch, for working
copied on to canvas or stiff white net and embroidered in
cross-stitch with the soft and exceptionally bright coloured
Saxon wools. Silks and wools might be used together in
Berlin work and beads as well to heighten the effect. As the
method of producing designs became more ingenious and
mechanical, with such short cuts as a single thread canvas
covered to look like silk to avoid working in the background,
designs tended to become cruder and less pleasing and the
violent colours of aniline dyes of 1858 hastened the decline.
However, with an artless wreath of roses or a bird pecking
a bunch of grapes, things could not go far wrong and some
of the simpler Berlin work is very pleasing. By the time it
had assumed the lumpish overblown characteristics shared
by the chintzes of the eighteen-seventies, William Morris's
band of enthusiasts and the example of the Royal School of
Needlework (founded 1855) were beginning slowly and surely
to turn embroidery design in quite another direction. (Fig. 23
shows a late example, draped over the back of an 1870-ish
chair.)

Holman Hunt's painting *The Awakening Conscience* shows
a typical piece of Berlin woolwork embroidery in progress.
With all its brilliant colours still in a ravel of loose ends, it
may be seen in the right foreground of the picture. This is
a gloriously typical Victorian drawing-room, the last word
in fashion, of the fifties. It was exhibited at the Royal
Academy of 1853 and, as Ruskin austerely remarked at the
time, there was nothing old or cherished in the room, all

was the latest, most frivolous and new. The room, typical of the drawing-rooms of the pretty stucco villas of St John's Wood built in the thirties and forties has something of the lightness and charm one would associate with Emma Place, but the furnishings of twelve years later have brought about a disastrous clutter. There is a confusion of hangings; muslin curtains overwhelmed with a heavy inner curtain, a large Japanese screen obscuring the wall. The pianoforte, almost touching the pedestal table, shares the same sharply cut, heavy and unnecessary carved ornament. The room still has pretty colours to commend it, but the whole effect is confused, like the clothes of the girl herself, fringed, swathed and draped in fussy elaboration.

Since Emma Place was sold in 1841, the Great Exhibition had happened, to fill the drawing-rooms of England with the newest novelties in occasional furniture. Detached from the claustrophobic profusion of upholstery and ornament in which they were originally placed, some of these novelties, despite the strictures of such as Eastlake and Ruskin, are very pretty and worth acquiring. Most of them, unlike dining-room pieces, are small enough in scale to fit into modern houses, but although small, are generally solid—indeed, almost comically robust, for their size. In occasional chairs there was wealth of fresh shapes, and *The Awakening Conscience* shows a particularly typical one, the Frenchified arm chair in which the girl's lover is sitting. The round-backed, waisted, fauteuil armchair with padded elbow rests is one of the most successful of Victorian chair shapes in all its variations. It looks comfortable and is comfortable and its satisfying rounded curves are ample enough to provide a good ground for embroidery or to show off buttoned and braided upholstery (Fig. 16). The chair in *The Awakening Conscience* is a very free adaptation of the French eighteenth century original. Some, however, particularly in the great country houses where the eighteenth century spirit lingered longest,

Fig. 16. Fauteuil occasional chair.

were near their originals—shorter in the leg and with higher
backs certainly, but carved, gilded or painted white, covered
in tapestry or petit point. The so-called *corset back* armchair
is a variation on the fauteuil theme, with cabriole legs (often
carved) and a substantial wide seat, padded elbow rests and
a tall, waisted back. The serpentine curves of the armchairs
annoyed the purists (particularly Eastlake) but they were
more comfortable and better looking than the romantic
baronial shapes taken from seventeenth century originals
which Eastlake for one preferred. High backed, remotely
reminiscent of Charles II chairs with their barley-sugar twisted
columns and carved crests, sometimes armed, sometimes
without, there were as many variations to this type as to the
French. The prettiest perhaps was the low fireside or sewing
chair; small, squarish, with upholstered back and seat and

somewhat stubby carved legs, but a perfect thing upon which to dispose a crinoline and a pleasing casual chair for today.

The Great Exhibition not only provided a stimulus for novel shapes but for novel materials; some of these—the cast-iron and brass furniture for example—were too outlandish for ordinary domestic purposes, except the ubiquitous brass or iron bedstead, but others were highly popular. Tunbridge ware or 'English mosaic' for example (made of small strips of veneer of various colours glued together and cut across in transverse sections), was especially favoured for small table tops and trays, and often worked into landscapes, with a surrounding pattern of marquetry.

Tunbridge ware by nature was not very practical save for flat surfaces and did not last out the whole period—by the sixties it had become ugly and mechanical—but papier mâché had a much wider application. The pieces shown at the Great Exhibition to demonstrate what papier mâché could do were perhaps too elaborate for general purposes—they included a complete pianoforte, the acoustics of which were highly unsatisfactory—but it made occasional furniture of a grace and delicacy which retained its prettiness right into late Victorian times. The process had first been introduced in the late eighteenth century from France and was perfected in the nineteenth by a firm called Jennens and Bettridge of Knightsbridge and Birmingham. Thick porous paper soaked in a solution of flour, glue and water and laid, three or four sheets together, in a metal mould, was dried out at a temperature of 90 to 100F. for about twelve hours. This was repeated until the required thickness was produced—an ordinary tea-tray only ¼" thick needed about ten layers—so that the making of a chair was a lengthy process. However Jennens and Bettridge, Spears of Oxford and various other firms found it worthwhile and made chairs and tables and other pieces finished with shellac, oil-polished and decorated with painting and inlay of mother of pearl made of nacreous shell and coloured woods. Spear's papier mâché had views of Oxford for its decoration, but most papier mâché was decorated with chinoiserie, exotic birds, landscapes or the bouquets of which the Victorians were so fond. Some of the painting was of a very high quality and the names of some of the artists—notably Edwin Haseler the flower painter and Frederick Newman, who was known for his peacocks—have been handed down. Examples decorated by them are particularly sought after.

Papier mâché has a rococo charm all its own. The chairs often have a frenchified cabriole leg, or slightly splayed tapering legs and lightly turned stretchers. As papier mâché is not particularly strong, chair seats are often made out of cane. Backs are shell shaped, either solid or open, often curved or with rococo convolutions but always fanciful and agreeably frivolous and light (Fig. 17, A and B). A beauty appears in the first picture of Augustus Egg's *Past and Present* series at the

Fig. 17. Chairs in papier mâché, c. 1850.

Tate. Trays, writing boxes (Fig. 18) and writing table furniture and all sorts of knick-knacks were made in papier mâché (the hand fire-screens of Plate 2 are an example. Small tables are especially attractive, particularly work-tables. The material was not durable enough to be entirely successful for large pieces.

Fig. 18. Writing box in papier mâché, with flower decoration in mother of pearl, c. 1860.

The Victorian drawing-room of the middle period was for the most part filled with a plethora of small pieces. Even so, the mania for belligerently large solid furniture was expressed in large cabinets and writing tables whose elaborate shapes made them almost as big as a piano, although their detail was minute and fussy. A popular piece was the *bonheur-du-jour*—a writing table and bureau combined. Third Empire French in origin as its name suggests, it had vaguely eighteenth century mouldings, was often ebonized and finished with brass mounts and might have painted panels, or insets of Wedgwood jasper ware. The writing table part lifted out on hinged supports, above was a tall centre compartment, sometimes mirrored and with tiers of drawers on either side. Display cabinets with large panels of plate glass, lined with velvet and made of mahogany, walnut and marquetry or buhl with ormolu mounts, or sometimes ebonized, were much more successful, being simple, horizontal shapes and often very handsome in a bulky way. Again, French in influence, often bow-fronted, the prettiest are medium sized or small ones (Figs. 19 and 20). The soft rose or crimson velvet flatters the most undistinguished china displayed in them and they make very nice small bookcases.

The drawing-room at this time was the room in which the lady of the house displayed her treasures—brackets and shelved overmantels were filled with ornaments. *Etagères* and *whatnots* were laden with examples of bijouterie or china Both these pieces were in essence tiered tables of about thirty inches high; the etagère generally oval or bow-ended and

Fig. 19. Mid-Victorian china cabinet in mahogany with ormolu mounts and rose-red velvet lining.

Fig. 20. Mid-Victorian display cabinet. Mahogany, inlaid, with ormolu mounts and crimson velvet lining.

having two or three tiers supported either by ormolu pillars or rococo brackets; the whatnot rectangular or square with spiral or bobbin shaped pillars and a drawer below. Both etagère and whatnots came in pairs, but pairs are rarely found and thus desirable. The *etagère* was a more elaborate and frenchified piece, often made in fancy woods such as tulip or king wood or satinwood (inlaid), having ormolu mounts and cabriole legs. Whatnots unfortunately became elaborate, set off with plush and decorated with fretwork towards the end of the period. However, they often still have a somewhat lumpish charm. Tiny objects of vertu would be displayed in table cases; rectangular, cabriole or tapered-legged tables in the fancy woods, often inlaid, the tops glassed over and lined with velvet or plush. These *bijouteries*, as they were called, are small and delicately made, the latest ones rather spindly. Without glass, lined with zinc, they might be used as *fern tables* and would be useful today for flower arrangement or indoor plants. Folios, magazines (or the novels which were coming out in weekly parts), and music might be stored in a *canterbury*. This is a most useful piece of furniture today—in essence a portfolio rack—with three or four dividing racks and a drawer or shelf underneath, standing on a short turned or pillared leg. They occur in walnut or in the

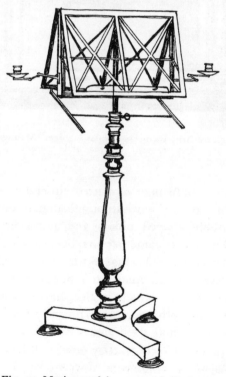

Fig. 21. Music stand in rosewood. Early to mid-Victorian.

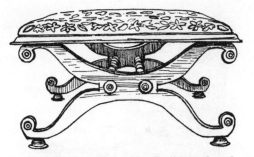

Fig. 22. Occasional stool c. 1860. Berlin wool-work seat.

French mode, inlaid with brass or ormolu bands. The most elaborate are of cabinet proportions the *music stand* and the occasional *stool* (often with Berlin woolwork seat) are other miscellaneous pieces. Both, being functional, are pleasingly plain (Figs. 21 and 22).

In the seventies the drawing-room suffered its most ugly period. Even then the beginnings of better things could be discerned, for Morris and Co., and the Century Guild were making and selling furniture, hangings and wallpaper to the minority of 'aesthetic' households, and their ideas, via John Ruskin's and Eastlake's nagging about good taste as a moral quality, were beginning to seep through to a wider public. Unfortunately, one of the first effects on ordinary furniture and decoration was to bring about a certain lack of nerve. The gaiety of earlier decades disappeared, colour became drab, timid. As far as furniture was concerned the battle of the styles went on, but renaissance and baronial drew ahead and the knobby, bobbin-turned legs, stretchers and back rails of chairs produced a peculiarly fussy and unwieldy appearance (Fig. 23). As for the buxom French style, the earlier amply upholstered curves had become stringy, the shapes over-elaborate and twisted. A Japanese influence on decoration made itself felt in the seventies. Bamboo occasional tables and other pieces

Fig. 23. Armchair c. 1870, with carpeted
back and seat, draped with Berlin wool-
work.

of furniture appeared, one of the most popular being the
ubiquitous Japanese screen. Oriental fans and Japanese pottery and porcelain and netsuke were added to the bric-à-brac
in the drawing-room.

The aesthetes had been looking to the orient for some time.
Rossetti collected blue and white oriental porcelain and in the
sixties Whistler was doing the same. In 1864 his *Princesse du
Pays de la Porcelaine* was exhibited—a willowy creature in
a rich kimono, the zig-zag lines of a Japanese screen behind
her, the whole composed with a lightness and sense of space
which was blessedly uncluttered. And the Japanese influence
did produce some pieces of furniture which were lighter in

Copper kettle: mid-nineteenth century. (*Buckland Abbey*).

'Dartmoor' copper kettle: probably mid-nineteenth century. (*Buckland Abbey*).

Copper gravy saucepan: mid- to late-nineteenth century. (*Buckland Abbey*).

Opaque glass rolling pin decorated with an inscription and flowers in colour and gilt: *c.* 1840. (*Buckland Abbey*).

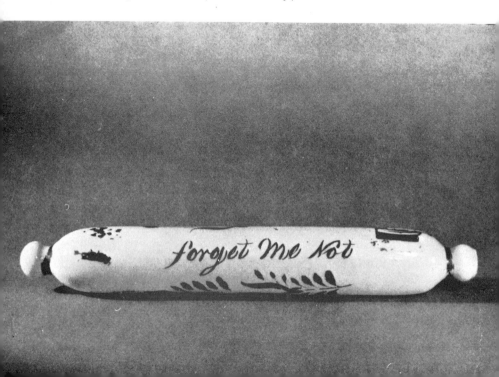

proportion, square and austere but restful to the eye compared with their ugly contemporaries. The *coffee table* (Fig. 24) in ebonized wood by E. W. Godwin, Whistler's architect, is an example. But the seventies and eighties are not a good period for the collector. Some of the Japanese screens are pretty enough in a fragile way, but frequently in very bad condition and difficult to repair. An early example of Japanese taste occurs in *The Awakening Conscience*.

Earlier Victorian screens, especially those decorated by stuck-on paper scraps might have the same charm as patchwork quilts and the same artless brightness but by the seven-

Fig. 24. Coffee table in ebonized wood (oak) by E. W. Godwin and made by William Watt, 1874.

D

ties and eighties amateur handwork was becoming boringly mechanical and the scraps were becoming drab and naturalistic. However a screen such as that from the Morris Gallery, Walthamstow, shown in Plate 3 was a portent. This was designed in 1884 by A. H. Mackmurdo (1851-1942) one of the founders of the Century Guild of Craftsmen (1883), trained originally at the Lambeth School of Art, a friend of John Ruskin and of William Morris. Its free design, flame-like and surprisingly abstract in character for its date, seems to owe something to Japanese influence, but the ideals that inspired it were those of Morris and the Pre-Raphaelites. Walter Crane, the graphic artist and designer, described the change that Pre-Raphaelite influence brought about: 'Plain white or green paint . . . drove graining and marbling to the public house. The simple old Buckinghamshire elbow chair, with its rush bottomed seat was substituted for the wavy-backed, curly legged and stuffed chair of the period—rich or simple flat pattern acknowledged the walls and expressed the proportion of the room. Blue and white Nankin or Delft routed Dresden or Sèvres from the cabinet. Plain oaken boards were preferred before the heavy mahogany.'

Above all, their most beneficial general effect was the reintroduction of the virtue of spaciousness. It was a lesson it took the English a long time to learn: even so by the nineties drawing-rooms were far less cluttered than those of the two decades before. There were two prevailing styles—reproduction eighteenth century (based on Adam for the most part, for the eighteen-nineties seemed to find an affinity with the seventeen-nineties) and the cultured contemporary style with Liberty or Morris or Century Guild fabrics and furniture which looked to Gimson and Voysey for inspiration.

The reproduction style of the nineties was of course the more prevalent. It was less austere and allowed far more frippery than the original Adam style which it emulated. It had a certain chintzy charm; sprigged chintz covered sofas and

easy chairs with deep flounces. The sofas had austerely high
backs by modern standards but were piled with silk damask
and velvet cushions. A light seat, with open back and sides to
seat two, was popular (Fig 25). This was a new shape, employing adapted late eighteenth century proportions. It might be
made in mahogany or in ebonized wood, the seat in brocade
or damask.

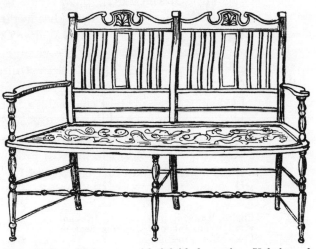

Fig. 25. Seat. Mahogany with inlaid decoration. Upholstered
in brocade, c. 1890.

Drawing-room chairs, either ebonized, mahogany or in
grand houses painted or gilded, were inspired by Adam and
his contemporaries. Sometimes they are spindly, their proportions too weedy. But some are charming. Fig. 26 shows an
example of the genre at its best, its inlaid flower ornament
unmistakably of its time and very characteristic. Chairs like
this belonged to drawing-rooms in which china cabinets displayed eighteenth century china (so often Worcester) against
light walls on which were hung muzzy romantic water
colours with gilt mounts and frames (perhaps by the lady

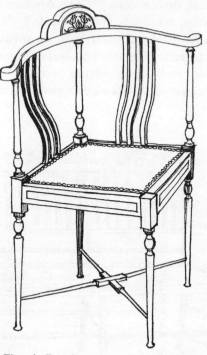

Fig. 26. Drawing-room chair. In ebonized wood, inlaid decoration. Seat in
brocade, c. 1896.

of the house), or the romantic aquatints of such as Angelica
Kauffmann or George Morland, in rather fidgety black and
gold frames.

Occasional tables were most often rectangular or square,
generally rather spindly in proportion, over high for their
thin legs, but well made in mahogany or inlaid after the
French style, and are still worth having. They lack the con-
viction of the earlier Victorian furniture, but light and small
as they are, fit well into a modern house.

The character of this reproduction style in the nineties
was however negative. It is at best a weedy Georgian with a

faintly nostalgic period flavour. The collector's pieces come from the Morris tradition. Such a one is the magnificent cabinet (Fig. 27) designed (c. 1899) by W. A. S. Benson and made by Morris and Co in rosewood inlaid with purple wood, tulip and ebony, with 'old silver' mounts. This lacks the conscientious uncouthness of earlier furniture by the Morris company, the self-conscious medieval style had disappeared and the problem of using metal with wood (which Eastlake never solved) has been mastered. The complicated running rhythms of the metal glazing bars have some of the freedom

Fig. 27. Cabinet of rosewood, inlaid and with 'old silver' mounts by W. A. S. Benson, c. 1899. Made by Morris & Co.

of art nouveau forms, without their exaggeration. This cabinet is sturdy and lacks the flimsiness which disfigured the contemporary 'period' style. This sturdiness brought a breath of country air into the drawing-room. Morris style drawing-rooms with their furniture, based on the old English provincial traditions of furniture making, lacked the frilly boudoir atmosphere of other Victorian drawing-rooms. Some of Walter Crane's book illustrations give an idea of them: bright soft colours, with blue and white china in the background, blue and white tiles around the hearth and tall chairs, perhaps modified ladder-backs in shape, black-painted, even rush-seated to give a dark accent of colour, to contrast with upholstered rather square armchairs, upholstered in a clear geranium red and a green Morris chintz. Such a room is the background to Walter Crane's version of *The Three Bears* in one of the Toy Books he did for Messrs Routledge. In other rooms the accent was provided by white rather than black, with white panelled walls rising to a low dado on which blue and white china was arranged. Against this setting the quiet beauty of wood, its texture and proportion could be really appreciated.

Against such a background Ernest Gimson's furniture showed at its best. Gimson and his partners, Sidney and Ernest Barnsley, produced furniture which was at once truly contemporary and rooted in tradition. Ernest Gimson had been trained as an architect at Leicester School of Art. The Gimson family were timber merchants in Leicester; hence, perhaps, his intuitive feeling for wood. Sidney and Ernest Barnsley—both architects, Sidney with Norman Shaw, Ernest with Sedding—he met when he was an architectural assistant with that fine church builder Edmund Sedding. Gimson had been introduced to Sedding by William Morris. All three were deeply influenced by Morris, so much so that Gimson dropped his architecture to be bound apprentice to a traditional pole-lathe chair-maker at Bosbury in the Cotswolds in order to learn to make things with his own hands, not merely draw designs for them. All three worked at the bench, hence their sensitive understanding of the character of the wood from which their furniture was made. The texture of a particular piece of wood was an integral element in the design. This awareness of texture was new. It was more than a sense of the peculiar fitness of a certain type of wood (which eighteenth century designers and the best of the early nineteenth century had shown); it was a difference in emphasis, in which the character of the wood itself determined the character of the resulting piece of furniture.

Gimson and Barnsley furniture was made in London under the name Kenton and Co, for two years. The firm first exhibited at the Morris-inspired Arts and Crafts Exhibition Society in 1890, where the cabinet reproduced in Fig. 28 was shown. But it was not a financial success and as they all wished to work in the country it was wound up and they retired to Pinbury in the Cotswolds, finally settling at Daneway House, which became Gimson's home. In the Cotswolds were craftsmen brought up in a vernacular tradition of furniture-making which had persisted since the seventeenth century, and smiths who could make locks and fittings. Using these craftsmen they founded a new tradition of craftsman-built furniture which has persisted until modern times. Gimson furniture was the sturdy forerunner of most good modern design.

Gimson's designs for drawing-room furniture seem more truly Victorian than most of his work, which really belongs to the twentieth century. Only his early pieces truly belong to our period. His cabinets are amongst his richest pieces. Of walnut inlaid with other woods they are much less austere than his strictly functional wardrobes, tables and bookcases. The inlay was sometimes used to give an all-over pattern—in one chevrons, in another stiffly branching dog roses, near enough to organic forms to produce a light and decora-

Fig. 28. Cabinet by Ernest Gimson, shown at the Arts and Crafts Exhibition of 1890 (from Aslin: *Nineteenth Century Furniture*).

tive effect, yet far from a tiresome, strained naturalism. Characteristic were the simple inlaid borders of bone or ebony and box, finishing off cornices, following the line of notched or chamfered legs. One very beautiful and elaborate cabinet stood upon legs of an elegant barley-sugar turning. The beauty of Gimson's furniture lies in the discreet rightness of its proportions allied to a richness of colour and texture in the wood used. Most at home in country interiors, his occasional tables, cabinets and chairs have a simple elegance that allows them to take their place honourably alongside the best antique or modern furniture.

CHAPTER IV

THE BEDROOM

THE VICTORIAN bedroom, looked back upon, has a particularly nostalgic charm. Four-post beds, or even brass beds with the firelight gleaming upon the knobs, suggest warmth and comfort. The appointments of the bedroom were unashamably devoted to upholstered comfort. With the exception of washstands, which always look gawky and slightly sordid, bedroom furniture almost throughout the entire period is worth the collector's attention.

Victorian beds—although there were some distressing examples shown at the Great Exhibition in 1851—can be particularly delightful. In 1841 at Emma Place the best bedroom had a 'Lofty carved Mahogany Pillar Four Post Bedstead, with Moreen furniture, fringed'. The early Victorian bed was a sturdy descendant of the Regency, very solid, very comfortable. (Emma Place boasted a feather bed, bolster and two pillows, as well as a pair of straw mattresses and a hair mattress). The moreen—a strong woollen material—would have made warm curtains when drawn, providing an almost airless cosiness. Less fusty was the *half-tester* which was popular in the forties and fifties—its bed-head adorned with a canopy and short curtains which came about a third down the bed when drawn, keeping the head and shoulders protected on frosty nights. This gradually ousted the four-poster bed. In 1875 Queen Victoria had a half-tester in her bedroom at Balmoral, but a bedroom, Lily Langtry's, which in 1899 was the height of fashion, had a four-poster once again. Half-testers and four-posters were made in mahogany, rosewood or walnut, posts and head deeply moulded or carved. They are heavily handsome and rather large for a modern house. For use in a small room half-testers can be cut down. The example shown is the foot-board of a half-tester, the head replaced by an upholstered modern head (Fig. 29). Not many of these beds survive, except perhaps in country house sales in deep country, but when found, because of their bulk, they are reasonable in price. Victorian four-posters are also rare. So many were cut up in the nineties, the pillars for use as stands for aspidistras or ferns in pots.

Much easier to accommodate are the metal beds. Brass and iron bedsteads were shown at the Great Exhibition, but the fashion for the open work metal bed with fabric hangings did not take hold until the late sixties and seventies. Eastlake's *Household Taste* of 1868 advocated such a bed as 'a change for the better' from the health point of view, looking back on

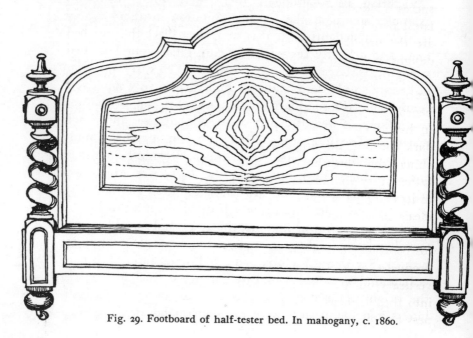

Fig. 29. Footboard of half-tester bed. In mahogany, c. 1860.

the time when 'night-capped gentlemen drew around their drowsy heads ponderous curtains, which bade fair to stifle them before the morning' and a 'huge four-poster was considered indispensable to every sleeping apartment'. Some of them, outrageously knobbed, were not an improvement on the majestic four-poster or the half-tester. Eastlake himself admitted this, denigrating 'lumpy bits of ornament' 'closely resembling a friendly group of garden slugs' on the intersecting joints. Some iron or brass beds, however, particularly the smaller ones, were light and pretty. Iron ones painted white, with their engaging curlicues, can look extremely pretty in a modern bedroom. Beds with curved ends are the most graceful, but a small rectangular brass bed in good order, draped with a due regard to texture and period, with candlewick or patch-work coverlet, has a country-bred freshness of its own. Eastlake's brass bedstead was one of his most successful designs, but the iron and brass bedsteads of the latest periods, when bedrooms were frankly light and frilly, are the prettiest. Fig. 30 A, B and C shows a selection of designs, one with its hangings in position.

The Pre-Raphaelites designed beds: Ford Madox Brown a set of cottage or farmhouse bedroom furniture. Rossetti's own bedroom at Cheyne Row, as drawn by Henry Treffry Dunn in his *Memoir*, shows a large four-poster bed, with heavy dark curtains, the firelight gleaming on the blue and white china decorating the walls—the whole a sumptuous cave of rather fusty comfort and magnificence. But Rossetti's house in its cluttered richness was no advertisement for the austere ideals in decoration advocated by Morris and Co. Morris's own granddaughter found the beds at Kelmscott too austere for comfort, but the simple, high-backed bed which the firm produced, with slender rails at head and foot with a strong vertical emphasis, brought a welcome simplicity and lightness into the bedroom. The new idea that open windows, freshness and light were necessary for health also contributed to

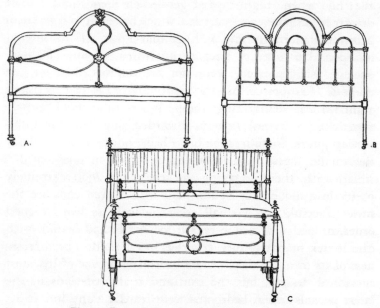

Fig. 30. Brass bedsteads, probably c. 1880-1890.

a new look in bedrooms. Book illustrations of the period show the trend; Walter Crane's *Red Riding Hood* interviewing the wolf in bed in a slender four-poster, with fresh white bed curtains sprigged with pale blue. Horrors could and did appear: some of the brass beds of the eighteen-nineties are monsters of ingenuity and ill-proportion, with hinged curtain poles, built like battle-ships for solidity; but the general tendency was towards a somewhat frilly and flimsy prettiness.

Bedroom chests, dressing-tables and wardrobes indeed became unpleasantly flimsy towards the end of the period. Apart from the beautiful chests designed by such as Gimson and Voysey, and the good reproductions of eighteenth-century mahogany which were just beginning to appear, this is a bad period. What was a welcome lightness in other pieces becomes a stringy meanness of proportion. Emma Place in

1841 had no bedroom chest of drawers: a Spanish mahogany wardrobe and a mahogany dressing-table with two drawers accompanied by a tray dressing glass, was all the storage afforded. A mahogany chest of the Emma Place period, however, is a highly desirable piece. Indeed the four-drawered chest of drawers hardly ever loses its sensible, sturdy charm right through from the forties to the eighties. Being purely functional it did not lend itself to misplaced ornament. The earliest pieces are most surely proportioned, perhaps, being nearest to the Georgian, but apart from unwieldy knob handles which may easily be replaced, the simple pieces keep their charm. A finely figured solid mahogany chest of the fifties is shown (Fig. 31, A), complete with its contemporary handles. With it is a more ambitious but less successful piece, also mahogany banded with veneer (Fig. 31, B). The attempt at architectural detail, with pilasters, is amusing but the proportions are not entirely happy. Incidentally, the simple piece is by far the better made, with drawers that run more easily and a sturdy construction which has stood up to hard use. Purely functional and designed for hard use is the military chest. This was a transportable piece, made in two sections which stand one upon the other, the top with two small drawers and one deep one, the bottom with two large drawers. With severely practical brass sunken handles, inset in neat rectangular brass plates, and brass-bound corners and key holes, made of good mahogany or cedar, it is a straight-forward piece of simple proportions, utterly plain but austerely handsome and perfectly at home in a modern room. It was apparently regulation until about 1870.

Victorian chests are amongst the most manageable of pieces. The wardrobe, often of mammoth proportions, is less easy. The magnificence of the Spanish mahogany wardrobe sold at Emma Place may be imagined: the wardrobes of the eighteen-forties were monumental in their proportions, made of fine timber and finished with simple if heavy mouldings at foot and cornice (Fig. 32). Sometimes the angles of their corners were rounded off. A fairy version of the early Victorian wardrobe was made in papier mâché, lined with cedar, inlaid with drooping bouquets of roses in mother of pearl. Although the unwieldy size of early Victorian wardrobes might seem

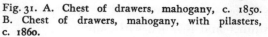

Fig. 31. A. Chest of drawers, mahogany, c. 1850.
B. Chest of drawers, mahogany, with pilasters,
c. 1860.

Fig. 32. Wardrobe. In mahogany, c. 1845.

to be against them at sales, they are becoming less easy to
find and perhaps because of their splendid timber, less reasonable in price. By the late sixties and seventies, the wardrobe
was collecting incrustations of unnecessary carving and elaboration. Eastlake, unfortunately, was one of those advocating
such embellishment, saying that with 'a few judiciously
introduced mouldings' the wardrobe might become a 'really
artistic feature'. His advice had unfortunate results. There
are a few seemly late Victorian reproduction Adam wardrobes about, but the frilliness of the bedrooms of the nineties
led to a plenitude of mirror glass and weedy husk decoration
inlay, so that good wood and workmanship was often spoiled
by weak and fussy design.

The Victorian dressing-table often has a gawky charm. Once again those of the forties are to be preferred. Emma Place boasted one with two drawers, in mahogany, completed by a tray dressing glass. These tray dressing glasses, a continuation from Georgian times, often heart-shaped, sometimes rectangular, are a trifle heavy compared with their late eighteenth prototypes, but still pretty and considerably cheaper in price. The Victorian dressing-table, on four solid carved and moulded legs, is frequently an awkward piece, even when of the early vintage (Fig. 33). It is best draped, to cover its

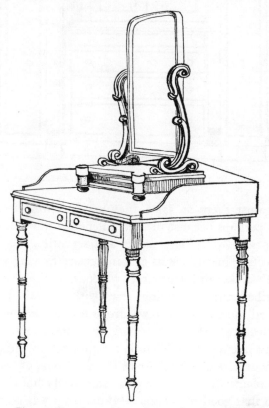

Fig. 33. Dressing table and tray dressing glass. In mahogany c. 1850.

Rockingham tea cup and saucer decorated in colour and gilt with roses and cornflower sprigs: *c.* 1840. (*City Art Gallery, Plymouth*).

Copeland tea service decorated with flowers and fruit in colour and gilt on an apple green ground: *c.* 1845. (*City Art Gallery, Plymouth*).

A – Vase with flower painting on a white ground and gilt: *c.* 1837-40. B – Inkwell encrusted with flowers in colour and gilt: Coalport *c.* 1840. C – Copeland vase with flower painting on shaded grey ground and gilt: *c.* 1840-45. D – Flower-encrusted pot and cover in colour and gilt: Coalport *c.* 1840. E – Vase with flower painting on a shaded grey ground and gilt; part of a garniture with C as the central vase: Copeland *c.* 1840-45. (*City Art Gallery, Plymouth*).

inevitable gauntness. The dressing mirrors sit more prettily upon a dressing chest. Full length dressing glasses, being purely functional, are worth having of all periods. Decently made of mahogany, often bobbin turned, adjustable, they are as useful as they are attractive. They do not appear very often in sales. The dressing-table went through a very nasty period during the late sixties and seventies; it was pretty again in the nineties, flounced in frilly draperies and by this time adorned with nostalgic toilet sets in beaten silver, covered all over with putti or *bocages* of incredible blossom. But by this time a looking glass had become attached and even the most restrained of Georgian reproductions has a glass poised unhappily (for the design at least) above it.

The basic needs of bed, dressing and storage once served, the Victorian bedroom varied greatly in the elaboration of the rest of its furniture. Some of the stateliest bedrooms had a sofa or chaise longue at the bottom of the bed. At Balmoral, the Queen's magnificent half-tester had an equally magnificent well-cushioned sofa at its foot. There were an assortment of chairs. The bedroom chair proper was a light occasional chair like a drawing-room chair, less elaborate and grand, and where the drawing-room chair was gilded, quite often merely painted white. Thonet's light bentwood chairs, first brought to this country for the Great Exhibition in 1851, made of beechwood steamed into curved shapes, utterly plain, modern-looking and functional, might well be used. The *balloon-back*, a drawing-room shape, popular from the forties to sixties, with an open curved or circular back, carved cross-piece or inset, in rosewood or mahogany, with upholstered seat and cabriole legs, also appeared as a bedroom chair, often with caned seat (fig 34, A and B). Amongst the simpler shapes were the 'nursery chairs' advocated by Eastlake in 1868 'of which the woodwork is stained black, with low seats and high backs' and of a shape retaining 'the spirit of an earlier and better style of work than is common in more

E

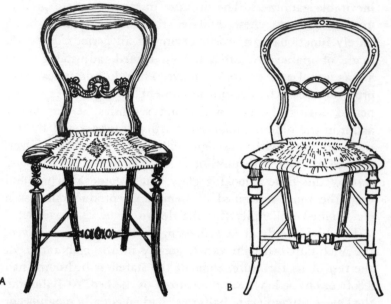

A

B

Fig. 34. Bedroom chairs, c. 1850. A. Mahogany, with carved splat.
B. Beech with bone inlay.

luxurious furniture'. In general, however, chairs followed
the drawing-room fashions throughout all phases of the
period, but plainer; if anything more spindly. Thus while
the chairs in Walter Crane's *Red Riding Hood* are substantial,
rush seated affairs, very much after the style of Eastlake's
'nursery chairs', the chairs in trade catalogues of the eighteen-
nineties are spindly beyond measure. Even a Mackintosh bedroom scheme looks etiolated as well as severe, the high backed
furniture too long-drawn out and unwelcoming[1] and, save for
a charming sofa and pretty Morris-like upholstery materials,

[1] Miss Aslin gives a photograph of a scheme by C. R. Mackintosh on
pl. 119 of her *Nineteenth Century Furniture*, and one by Liberty's
(pl. 107). The Mackintosh room is surprisingly modern, but rather clinical,
c. 1899. The Liberty room suggests a tradition followed faithfully well
into recent years by good but sad seaside boarding houses.

the scheme by Messrs Liberty (1897) is very weedy and thin in its furniture shapes.

Of the *washstand* the less said the better. Never an object of beauty, when treated in a monumentally gothic style (c. 1875) as at Castell Coch, near Cardiff by William Burges, it is at least an amusing set-piece, but Eastlake's efforts to make it plainer made it even more sordid and set a traditional pattern in horrible washstands that lasted into the nineteen-twenties. A good marble top, however, is very worth having, among other things it makes an excellent kitchen table-top for cooking upon. Washstands at local sales are often worth buying for their marble alone.

These are the basic elements of the Victorian bedroom's furnishing. But there was an enormous variation in the degree of elaboration in bedroom furnishings. The Emma Place bedroom was very pleasant and quite relatively simple compared with the elaboration of, for example, Lily Langtry's bedroom in the eighteen-nineties. Bedrooms of this kind were furnished almost as sitting-rooms, with occasional tables (such as Fig. 35), easy chairs and so on.

A useful piece of furniture often consigned to bedroom or schoolroom was the *davenport*. This is a piece particularly worth having today—small in scale, pretty and useful. It is in effect a writing desk and tiny chest of drawers for odd-ments combined, with sloping leather covered writing top and deep drawers right down each side of its solid looking body to a moulded foot. Early examples are neater in their proportions and detail, but fashion did not alter the daven-port much and it keeps its charm throughout the period. Unfortunately, because it is so pretty and so useful for a small house—rarely much over 3′ high and about 2′ 6″ across the top—the davenport is greatly in demand and therefore expensive.

Bedside or chamber pot cupboards the Victorians also did rather well. These are generally very plain, simple cupboards,

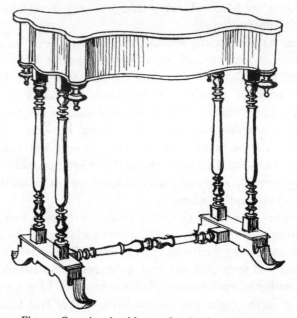

Fig. 35. Occasional table, c. 1850-60. In mahogany.

sometimes with a serpentine front and frequently of a particularly good mahogany. As with all functional furniture,
they are nicely proportioned.

Several incidental bedroom furnishings are interesting and
worth collecting. Bed covers are particularly interesting—the
traditional patchwork or ordinary quilt especially so—with
an entire lore of their own. The patchwork quilt was a rural
thing and they were treasured in the farm houses for years.
They belong rather to the eighteenth-forties than to later
on. Millais painted two Academy pictures of his little girls
in bed in 1866, *Sleeping* and *Waking*. In one a small quilted
satin coverlet is shown (*Sleeping*), in the other a white croch-
eted cover with deep silk fringe and a bold texture-pattern.
Later Victorian bed covers of this kind are beginning to be
sought after and to command a price. In the *Waking* picture

the child sits up in a very pretty but simple nursery iron bed and the large white patterned bed cover gives an air of richness to the effect. Even the snowy white lace bedspreads of the nineties are no longer despised. The modern return to frilly bedroom interiors is bringing Victorian bedcovers into favour again and as they were a rather expendable type of possession (with the exception of the patchwork quilts perhaps), they are understandably rare. Only in country places, where the fashion has not yet arrived, are they likely to be acquired at bargain prices.

CHAPTER V

THE KITCHEN

THE RICHNESS of Victorian life was founded solidly upon a good kitchen. In fact the kitchen had a whole civilization of its own. Its relics are worth collecting, for it was a time when food was not only of excellent quality, but cooked and served with the greatest care. 'Trifles make perfection' Mrs Beeton said. Her recipes had each 'claimed minute attention'. The tools of such a careful craft are pleasing things. Functional, trimmed sometimes with a peasant gaiety they are typical of the best of Victoriana.

The kitchen at Emma Place must have been a very pleasant part of the house. The early nineteenth century stucco houses round Stoke and Devonport have important kitchens and cool larders, with floors paved with slate, and in the larders a slate slab on which food was kept wonderfully cold. The focal points of the kitchen were the great table, with a scrubbed wood top and thick baluster legs often painted black, with drawers below, and the range, shiny with stove black, between which the cook moved at her work. A generous built-in dresser and cupboards completed the essentials of the room. The back-kitchen or scullery with sink and copper for boiling clothes was used for the humbler arts of preparing vegetables and laundering. At Emma Place the large kitchen had two tables, one large one with drawers for kitchen knives and tools. There were four rush-seat chairs, a kitchen clock, 6 tea trays, two mats and 'pieces of carpet' and the range was finished off with a 'kitchen fender'.

Kitchen furniture throughout the period did not change

very much, except perhaps to receive the plainer out of fashion pieces from above stairs. The 'rush-seat chairs' of basically eighteenth century design would have lasted until the end of the century, when a type of them, the 'Sussex' chair, was elevated to dining-room status by William Morris's influence. They were of a type constantly advocated in vain by Eastlake, who considered their lines much superior to the frivolities of fashionable furniture. Pictures of cottage kitchen interiors by Condy and the like *genre* painters show ladder-backs or Windsor-type chairs, probably made in beech. In cottage kitchen furniture later in the century, locally made chairs follow basically Georgian traditions of design, with a slight trace of contemporary fashion in the detail. Fig. 36 shows

Fig. 36. Kitchen armchair. In beech. c. 1860.

an armchair (perhaps made c. 1860) from a Cornish kitchen and typical in its large plainness. These honest, plain pieces scarcely distinguished enough for antique shops, turn up locally at country sales and are worth looking for in junk shops.

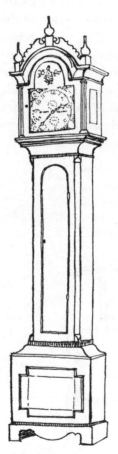

Fig. 37.
Longcase clock by a Berkshire maker, c. 1840. In mahogany.

The kitchen clock at Emma Place was probably a plain long-case clock. These had not changed much, save in the detail of face and a new plain heaviness in the mouldings, since the eighteenth century. The local maker's name which appears on the face now only means the assembler and stockist. The example in Fig. 37 bears the name of a Berkshire assembler and dates from the eighteen-forties. The painted faces and lettering have a folk art cheerfulness. Later in the century (c. 1860) something like the American pub clock might be seen, with a round face, in a short case in which it hung on the wall, with elaborate and bright painting on glass below the dial, going perfectly with the rather spiky mid-nineteenth century figures on the clock face. The tea trays at Emma Place may have been plain functional wooden ones, but from the eighteen-forties onwards there were the most lovely papier mâché ones, varying from the consciously chaste pseudo-classical designs to rococo confections inlaid with mother of pearl.

The fender to the range was probably made locally. Some of the most pleasing details of houses built in the years of mining prosperity in the South West are the work of local foundries. Bootscrapers, door stops, the heads of down spouts were made by them. Fig. 38 shows a rampant lion doorstop of about 1850.

Kitchen metalware of the Victorian age was always decorative. Gothic detail which on porcelain or over elaborate furniture was tiresome, became decorative and only slightly absurd on a copper cake or jelly mould. Victorian food, highly seasoned and garnished was always sumptuously produced

Fig. 38. Lion doorstop. In cast iron, painted black, c. 1850 made by St. Blazey Foundry, Cornwall.

and as Mrs Beeton said, 'every proper acompaniment to a dish' should be 'served with it'. Mrs Beeton's *Every Day Cookery and Housekeeping Book* of 1871 in its 'Dictionary of Cookery' gives wood engravings of the appropriate moulds for everything, puddings, soufflés, raised pies, even cakes. The shapes are remarkable pretty. Plate 4 shows two moulds, one a pudding, the other a ring mould for jelly. Mrs Beeton describes an open jelly, with whipped cream 'flavoured with sherry and sweetened with pounded sugar' piled high in the centre. 'The jelly should be made of rather a dark colour to contrast nicely with the cream.' Mrs Beeton is much concerned with the aesthetic effect: a cut of a rather gothic mould accompanies a receipt for a jelly in two colours, red and very pale sherry, and the result looks oddly like layered glass. The pudding mould illustrated has the mark of its makers, Evans and Matthews of Birmingham, near the base. Plate 6 shows a low open mould of the type used for creams, the kind of pudding which, with six eggs and one and a half pints of cream in the ingredients, makes Victorian food sound rich and lavish. By the seventies moulds were also made in earthenware, pewter and tin, none of them as decorative as copper. Another piece of kitchen metalware decorative in itself is the pestle and mortar—for so many ingredients in the Victorian kitchen had to be pounded by hand. But perhaps most attractive are the copper kettles—still traditional in shape (Plates 6 and 7). The larger kettle is known as a 'Dartmoor' kettle.

Mrs Beeton gives a receipt for making butter into elegant curls before it is sent to the table. In country households where the butter was made it was sent out from the dairy ornamented with flowers, fern leaves or shells. The ornamental moulds are charming in themselves and beautifully carved and made. Two are illustrated in Fig. 39. Other wooden moulds are worth a search. Apple marmalade tart, according to Mrs Beeton was best ornamented by a 'paste-mosaic'.

Fig. 39. Butter moulds. In sycamore wood.

This was achieved by rolling the pastry on to a mould pro-
cured from the turner 'a board with designs upon it representing various ornamental matters'. This sort of decorative
work was a vestige of the craft tradition which had produced
the sycamore-wood moulds for ginger bread biscuits at the
country fairs.

But some very attractive 'treen' was produced for the
Victorian kitchen, from turned pepper mills to comely wooden
spoons and the 'spotless wooden bowl' in which the lady of
the house washed up the breakfast things, a task, according
to Mrs Beeton, carried out in some old families as a relic of
the old puritan system.

Some of the cooking vessels themselves are very attractive.
At Emma Place there was a copper 'Turbot Kettle' and a
'Bell Metal Skillet'. Sleek copper cooking pans of the period
are most handsome. Plate 8 shows a small copper saucepan

of the type illustrated by Mrs Beeton for melting butter or gravy. It is a rather nicer one than Mrs Beeton's, with its elegant turned wooden handle. Amongst the other kitchen metalware at Emma Place was a 'Bed Candlestick and Snuffer'. In nearly all pictures of Victorian kitchens this is kept with the tinder box on the shelf above the hearth and the simple brass candlestick, with its nightcap-like snuffer attached, can have pleasing if solid proportions.

It is amongst the 'sundry China', the pitchers, bread pans, '6 Stone Jars', dishes and earthenware that some of the most charming things in the Victorian kitchen may be found. Some very decorative nineteenth-century earthenware was a kitchen speciality. 'Mocha' ware for example, also a fine brown stoneware and 'cloam' earthenware. Mocha was made from c. 1785 until its production petered out in the nineteen-hundreds, but it hardly appeared elsewhere than in the kitchen or public house and has only recently reached antique shops—perhaps because it was reckoned so cheap and expendable that it was not worth the cherishing. With a fine earthenware ground of drab, later white, it had bands of deep coffee colour, thinner bands of blue and either a 'run' decoration, forming a dark brown feathery pattern which could be seaweed, feathers or moss, or sometimes an all-over marbling between lines of colour. This 'Mocha' was pre-eminent all through Victoria's reign for tankards, large and small jugs, covered dishes, washing up bowls and other useful ware.

The 'sundry Earthenware' mentioned in the Emma Place kitchen, where it has survived, is also worth collecting. All through the nineteenth century local potteries were at work, producing 'cloam' or unglazed or partly glazed earthenware pitchers, bread pans, pots and jars which have a noble traditional outline, purely functional, plain and uncluttered. These vary in their quality, but one particularly noble ware was produced by the North Devon potters, working in the

Barnstaple-Bideford area with the Fremington clay and the local white pipe-clay. As well as their ordinary 'cloam' for everyday use they produced the so-called Harvest pottery, glazed slip ware, jugs and jars, mostly presentation pieces with appropriate names and inscriptions drawn in the slip, along with figures at the plough, or sailing ships, compasses, mermaids, birds, flowers, roses, tulips and butterflies. The decoration, cut away in parts, or scratched to reveal the dark body beneath, is conceived so much in the style of comparable pots made in Anne's or George I's reign that it is almost a shock to read dates like 1845, on the inscriptions. These hand-some pitcher-shaped jugs, made for cider or ale, show the persistence of local tradition, with no self-conscious anti-quarianism about it, from early eighteenth to mid nineteenth century without a break. A similar peasant pottery tradition lingered in North Wales and Sussex. There is a fine small collection of harvest ware, where eighteenth-century pots may be compared with the later examples, in the Folk Museum at Buckland Abbey.

Harvest pottery is rare because it was cherished, the cloam and kitchen stoneware because it has been broken, or dis-regarded as old-fashioned and thrown away. But large cloam crocks to hold bread (the nicest of bread pans is a cloam pan with butter yellow glaze inside and a white scrubbed wood lid with a hand grip) occasionally turn up; also water pitchers and the big jars with handles a little like Roman oil jars in which bacon was salted, or eggs pickled. The '6 stone jars' at Emma Place may have been the dark brown glazed two handled ones in which (in the South West at any rate) pil-chards were marinated—packed tight with bay leaves, spices and vinegar, covered in by the neatly knobbed lid. These jars, decorated simply with incised lines and impressed bands of pattern make delightful flower vases. They were indispen-sable in the kitchen interiors of the eighteen-forties and in an Academy picture of 1874 one stands on top of a cup-

board in the foreground. Fig. 40, A shows one from an old
house in Stoke, Devonport, where it spent its last days hold-
ing flour. Rather pleasing but more crude stoneware jars were
also used for the storage of gin and spirits.

Liquor had a certain place in the Victorian kitchen. Mrs
Beeton, most moderate and abstemious of women, discusses
the allowance of ale to be handed out below stairs (a pint a
day of ale or stout for a female servant, for no girl could
be expected to do hard physical work on less, she said), and
gives receipts which involve wine and spirits. Her 'Invalid
Cookery' has a brandy receipt 'for cases of extreme exhaus-
tion' which sounds rather delicious, and rum and milk, to be

Fig. 40. A. Stoneware kitchen jar. Deep
brown glaze and incised decoration, Mid-
nineteenth century or later. B. Milk jug,
in white, decoration in colour and gilt
and inscription 'No Place Like Home';
Staffordshire.

taken every day before breakfast must have been fresh and reviving. Mrs Beeton recommends that the ale should be bought in casks. She might also have advocated the very pretty Staffordshire spirit casks that were made early and late in the period, each with a tap and its title embellished in gilded letters; those with hunting scenes transfer-printed in colours, belonging to the last decades of the century. But the tradition of a robust gaiety lingered long and, commercialized though they are, these little barrels are very decorative (Fig. 41, A, B and C).

Some very delightful glass bottles and flasks with moulded decoration which is delightfully naïf and spirited were made in America during the period. These, from the Wistar factory and from the Stoddard, New Hampshire factory and others, are avidly collected today; they had several very effective patterns, such as the Sunburst. They also produced very nice spirit flasks imitating the decorated base metal powder flasks of the time. Nothing of the same kind survives in England, the nearest to it in spirit being the glassware that the glass blowers of the local factories made for their own amusement —the 'friggers'—twisted glass walking sticks, opaque glass rolling pins and the like. The Nailsea tradition was in decay by the time Victorian's reign began, but its spirit flasks, can just be counted as Victoriana. Plate 9 shows one, eighteen-fortyish in style, inscribed with the usual romantic message.

Kitchen ware also in a sense were the horn beakers and

Fig. 41. Spirit casks. Pottery, with ivory white glaze.
A and C, c. 1890, decorated with coloured transfer prints.
B. c. 1860, decorated with a wreath of flowers in gilt.

Fig. 42. A. Horn beaker. Silver mounts and inscription ' Thomas Gray '. B. Horn beaker. Silver mounts and initials C.H.H. c. 1840.

pewter tankards of the era. The beakers, of varying size, were made of cow's horn, sometimes very beautifully marked. They are occasionally mounted in silver (they were given as prizes for rural sport) as is the specimen dated 1840 in Fig. 42. They are quietly beautiful things to collect, completely simple in shape, relying for their decoration on the variations in the horn colour, which can be almost white through amber to a deep blackish brown. Pewter tankards, often initialled, for kitchen or pub use, are much more antique looking than their actual dates suggest, this being a class of metalwork in which the eighteenth century designs stayed long.

Seahorse and shell vase or sweetmeat made by Belleek: late nineteenth century. (*City Art Gallery, Plymouth*).

A – Pastille burner in the form of a castle – in white finished with colour and gilt: Rockingham type. B – Sheep: Rockingham type but perhaps made by a Staffordshire factory. C – Poodle on a wine-coloured cushion with golden tassels: Rockingham. All are *c.* 1840. (*City Art Gallery, Plymouth*).

Plate with black transfer decoration: Staffordshire 1841. (*City Art Gallery, Plymouth*).

Stoneware jug in white with cast relief decoration: impressed with the mark of the Union Pottery and with patent stamp for 1861. (*City Art Gallery, Plymouth*).

CHAPTER VI

VICTORIAN CHINA: PORCELAIN
AND POTTERY

ALL THE characteristics of Victorian taste are to be seen fully
developed in their pottery and porcelain, and most attractively, for not only did the Victorians inherit a great tradition
of proportion and craftsmanship from the eighteenth-
century factories but they had themselves a peculiar genius
for small things. Like the Elizabethans they had a feeling
for minute details whilst their sense of scale in their large
projects was poor. Victorian palaces, like the Elizabethan ones
which they so often copied in style, are an uncomfortable
assemblage of fidgety detail. The engineers—such as Brunel
—preserved a sure sense of mass, but those who built for
pleasure lacked this. With porcelain, in its inherent character
meant to be small, decorative, elaborate, they were more
successful. Pottery, fundamentally useful and plebeian, like
Victorian engineering, could be very good when 'penny-
plain'. Only when it sought to emulate the elaboration of
porcelain did it become unpleasing.

The characteristics of the early, middle and late Victorian
period in pottery and porcelain are perhaps less easily
defined than in other Victoriana. For although eighteenth-
century proportion—the inheritance of the classical vase shape
—lingered long, the lowest ebb of taste, the bleak period of
the eighteen-seventies, also affected porcelain. Pottery suffered:
weak, staggering patterns, fussy proportions, spoil late Victorian earthenware and china; and porcelain, made for a

plutocratic minority declined into a horrible quest for technical novelty. Along with the pursuit of technique for its
own sake there was decline into painting of a mawkish realism
(just bearable in flower and bird subjects, less so in sentimental figures), but proportions were relatively less affected
and workmanship remained excellent. In the last decades
of the nineteenth century charm disappeared, replaced by a
conscientious and serious minded approach to beauty. The
Japanese vogue and the imitation of oriental models brought
its own disciplines. Those movements perhaps least attractive
to twentieth-century eyes, cleared the way for the artist-
potters who were the forerunners of the great twentieth-
century English artist potters. The Pre-Raphaelites influenced
porcelain less than they did pottery, but their rediscovery
of pre-eighteenth-century modes, their insistence on craftsmanship as more than a material way of life, influenced both
porcelain and pottery.

The first period of Victorian porcelain, as in all Victoriana,
produced the greatest number of attractive pieces. It was
most close to the eighteenth-century tradition. Not only the
Worcester and Derby factories inherited eighteenth-century
standards but Coalport took over from Caughley (where John
Rose had served his apprenticeship), Nantgarw and Swansea,
while Copeland's succeeded Spode. Minton's (founded in 1793)
was begun by an engraver, Thomas Minton, who had worked
at Caughley, and for Adams, Wedgwood and Spode. Many
of the smaller factories which arose in Staffordshire had
eighteenth-century origins. Perhaps porcelain of the eighteen-
forties looked back too much to be characteristic of the fully-
developed Victorian taste, but it is to this link with the earlier
period that its owes its peculiar freshness and charm. In
domestic ware characteristic shapes echoed those of silver.
Increased mastery over materials brought new elaboration
and a certain uncertainty in proportion: the tea-pots of the
eighteen-forties are uneasy rococo, echoing the waisted,

c. 1840

1851

c. 1865

c. 1890

Fig. 43. Typical teapot shapes. Early mid- and late Victorian.
c. 1840, Rockingham type. 1851, Worcester: exhibited at the Great
Exhibition. c. 1865, Worcester, jewelled ware. c. 1890, Staffordshire.

horizontal emphasis of the tea-kettle rather than the old comfortable pseudo-classical helmet shape of the teapot of the
eighteen-hundreds. Instead of coming solid to the base, the
teapot most often stood upon a moulded foot, its body shaped
with a serpentine curve (Fig. 43). Cream jugs and sauce boats
of a fattened eighteenth-century shape stood upon four feet
(imitating Sèvres) upon a heavily moulded base; sugar bowls,
slop basins and the larger plates, or the comports of dessert
services, had elaborately moulded edges, sometimes of open-
work, generally gilded. Ogee curves abounded. Cups opened
so wide at the rim as to cool tea poured into them almost
immediately. Plate 10 shows a pretty sprigged cup and saucer
of the forties with this fault. Both domestic ware and decorative pieces, such as vases, were heavily gilded and most often
decorated by a deep, rich ground colour, reserving gilded
panels of finely painted flower and fruit bouquets, exotic
birds, or even Watteauesque figure subjects. Vases retained
the characteristic classical 'Pompeian Mortuary Urn' shape
(as one writer about 1845 so attractively described it) which
had come in with the Greek revival at the beginning of the
century and which was to persist, weakened sometimes by
variations (cf. vase in revived rococo (c. 1850) Fig. 44) and
improvements, until its close.

The charm of the porcelain of the eighteen-forties rests
mostly upon its rich colours, fine painting and soft gilding.
Technical improvements brought about the characteristically
rich ground colours. Coalport had introduced a maroon in
1821 and by 1849 had two greens—the Sardinian (deep) and
the victorian (pale)—a rich underglaze blue (Bleu du Roi),
a pale turquoise and a pink (Rose du Barry, 1849). Copeland's
was noted for the softness and evenness of their ground colouring on the fine bone-china base (first made by Josiah Spode II
1754-1827) and for their flower painting. Plate 11 illustrates
a tea-service attributed to Copeland. Shape and style are
typical of the eighteen-forties. The ground is a soft apple

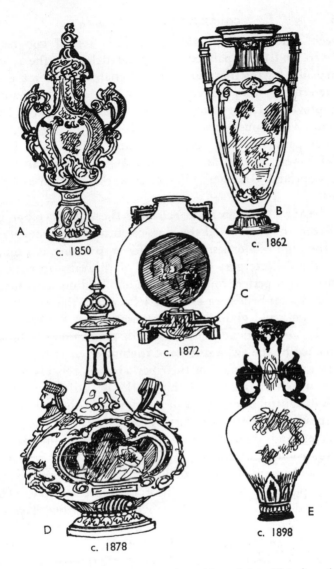

A c. 1850

B c. 1862

C c. 1872

D c. 1878

E c. 1898

Fig. 44. Typical vase shapes. Early, mid- and late Victorian. A. c. 1850, revived rococo. B. c. 1862, classical style. C. c. 1872, the Japanese taste. D. c. 1878, renaissance—one of the 'Potter' vases. E. c. 1898, misty flower painting, applied tinted clay ornament.

green and it and the gilding perfectly set off bouquets of flowers and fruit, painted with great delicacy—the roses in particular having that thoroughbred charm found in the early nineteenth-century flowers, soon to be lost by horticultural 'improvers'. The style of painting is much like that of David Evans, who must have influenced many of the Copeland flower painters. This exquisite painter, best known for his wild flowers, worked first for the Swansea factory, afterwards for Copeland, Grainger's Worcester works, Minton and Coalport.

The three vases in Plate 12 shows the uneasy compromise between the rococo and the classical urn shape characteristic of the eighteen-forties. But the flower painting is exquisite and the delicate grey backgrounds of the vases to right and centre are a perfect foil for flowers and gilding. Less successful is the fat-bellied vase to the left, where the brilliance of the flowers and gilding are overpowering set against a completely white ground. The uncertain proportion of the vase is echoed by the awkwardness of the flower encrusted covered vases or pots, so typical of their period and probably by Coalport, who was famed for this work. Beautifully modelled, with delightful colour, their proportion lacks the restraint and sureness of eighteenth-century rococo.

Vases and domestic ware in the eighteen-forties were decorated by flower and fruit bouquets (both more naturalistic and more highly coloured than eighteenth-century flower painting) or topographical or figure painting. Topographical subjects were a hangover from earlier days—the discreet black and white houses in a landscape of Regency Liverpool and Worcester. A Chamberlain Worcester dish with a view of Witley Court (reproduced in Mr Godden's *Victorian Porcelain*, p. 135, Plate 66) c. 1845, has the familiar landscape with its Palladian mansion surrounded by a richly gothic, deep gilded border of trefoil shapes—purely Victorian in character and the battle of the styles exemplified. Vases, par-

ticularly at Chamberlain's Worcester factory, were produced
with rich grounds and gilding, setting off painted figure scenes,
reminiscent of the *genre* subjects taken from romantic literature and history shown on canvas at the Royal Academy each
year. This figure work was stylized enough not to be irritating,
as the later furious quest for naturalism was.

Even figure work in the parian was stylized to a certain
degree. It strove for classical idealism rather than naturalism.
Unglazed figures, left in the biscuit state, had been made in
the late eighteenth century (cf. some charming Derby figures)
but the rage for parian 'statuary' really began in the forties,
with the composition of a body originally invented at the
Copeland works, which was supposed to have the character
of marble. Incidentally, it is most likely that it was invented
by an ex-Derby workman[1] although the figures so produced
could not have been less like the Derby figures in spirit. The
intention was not a porcelain figure as such, but a reasonably
priced imitation of full size statuary. Pieces exhibited at the
R.A. were reproduced in parian and Royal Academician
sculptors commissioned to design subjects for it. Single figures
and groups were produced, one the *Return from the Vintage*,
(Copeland), actually consisting of seven figures. Copeland's,
Minton and Wedgwood all made parian, marketing it under
different names—Copeland's called it 'statuary porcelain',
Minton's 'Parian', and Wedgwood 'Carrara'. Copeland's
were the first firm to produce it, Minton's following on
(c. 1847), but by the 1851 exhibition Grainger's Worcester
factory, Meigh, Wedgwood, Coalport, Bell of Glasgow, and
several others were exhibiting parian. Parian of the forties
was confined to figure groups, a few elaborate Copeland figures
—supported centrepieces, with the figures in statuary, the
comport glazed, gilded and enamelled. Potts of Birmingham
(1848) used Copeland figures (mostly after models by Woolner)
in parian with metal mounts of brass, bronze, electro-silvered

[1] See Godden: *Victorian Porcelain* pp. 150-151.

or gilt for candle lamps, vases, gas brackets and so on. Copeland's also produced moulded reproduction hellenistic vases
in the material as early as 1846.

The 1851 Exhibition showed Victorian porcelain at the
height of its elaboration. Most characteristic of porcelain of
the fifties was the passion for Sèvres. The vogue for the French
fashion in furniture was echoed in porcelain. Coalport ' Sèvres '
imitations were good enough to deceive the directors of the
firm themselves.[1] Minton and Copeland, both for vases and
domestic ware, also followed the Sèvres fashion. Simpering
pseudo-Watteau figure subjects decorated vases of a simpler,
more elegant proportion than those of the forties. The Sèvres
style was elaborate, not to say fussy in detail, but the general
proportions were good, coming straight from eighteenth-
century models. The Sèvres ground colours were faithfully
reproduced and there was gilding of a sumptuous richness,
sometimes a little overpowering and with a hard, mechanical
quality compared with the less technically perfect eighteenth-
century examples. The painted panels were often delightful:
the figure subjects of Thomas Allen for Minton brought a
certain mid-Victorian charm, very English, to the elaborate
foreign-looking vases, whilst Jesse Smith did the most delicate
roses, for Coalport William Cook added elaborate and slightly
mannered flower and fruit compositions, and John Randall
both exotic birds in a careful reproduction of the Sèvres style
and spirited and naturalistic bird studies in the same tradition
as the illustrated natural histories of the period. In the fifties,
the flower, fruit and birds *genre* and flowers copied from
Sèvres, were the main subjects decorating china. But there
was also a restrained and slightly stiff classical style of decoration, in part deriving from Sèvres, but very Victorian in
character. R. F. Abraham of Coalport's painted figure subjects in this style, and for Worcester, Thomas Bott and

[1] The disguise was made effective by a reproduction of the Sèvres
mark.

Abraham Callowhill. Thomas Bott in fact started an entirely new technique—the so-called 'Limoges' decoration which reproduced in porcelain the effect of the bright dark blue background and stark white figures of the Limoges enamels of the Renaissance. His figures, in the softened Victorian version of the classical, have a certain sentimental dignity, much appreciated by the Prince Consort and by Queen Victoria herself, who often chose pieces to give away as presents. Set plain against their dark backgrounds, enclosed within a severely restrained classical border and painted upon wares which faithfully reproduced classical Greek proportions, they are amongst the most nobly plain of all Victorian design. Worcester's jewelled ware of the eighteen-fifties and sixties with Callowhill's classical heads in vignettes set in porcelain studded all over with little gilded knobs, is fussy and over-rich by comparison (Fig. 43, C). By its nature, porcelain could not reflect the battle of the styles found in other departments of the Great Exhibition. The Gothic, save in richly gilded borders with trefoil or other vaguely gothic motives (as in a Coalport dessert plate shown in 1851, with a sumptuous fruit piece painted in the middle and deep gothic border) was not appropriate to the material.[1] But the trend of decoration in the fifties and sixties was increasingly naturalistic and imitative. Flowers and birds might have come from the botanical illustrations of the period. Royal Academy pictures were reproduced by the enamel painter in miniature on vases; for example J. M. W. Turner's classical subjects by Daniel Lucas on vases for Copeland's (Fig. 44, B). The most successful pieces were direct reproductions of Sèvres or work produced by a factory—such as Derby—which had a conservative tradition still owing much to the eighteenth-century. Derby figures of the eighteen-sixties preserved their eighteenth

[1] Although Pugin did design thoroughgoing Gothic decoration, both printed and painted, for Minton's who exhibited it in the Great Exhibition group.

century style; indeed they were taken from the old moulds and despite a subtle softening of the original, giving them a Victorian air, have more decorative value than the parian which was all the rage during the period of the Great Exhibition.

There was a great output of parian during the fifties. It was obviously exhibition material. Royal Academy sculpture was reduced by Cheverton's ingenious reducing machine to the size of manageable ornaments for the middle class home. Elaborate groups appeared and many Etty-like chastely plump classically draped female figures; such as Copeland's *Ino* by J. H. Foley, shown at the 1851 exhibition and *Miranda* (c. 1850) by John Bell for Minton's. Literary subjects such as the *Faust and Margaret* by Kirk for Worcester (Kerr and Binns) and the Worcester dessert service in parian and porcelain with figures from *A Midsummer Night's Dream*, appeared. The 'Midsummer Night's Dream' set was a portent. The parian decoration in relief against a tinted body—classical motif surrounding cameo like medallions and the Greek form of the comports—like a Greek drinking cup incongruously supported on a column above the parian statuary base on which Bottom and Snug disport themselves, shows that pre-occupation with classical form and with texture which was to interest the next two decades.

Instead of the gay painting and gilding of the fifties, porcelain became increasingly solemn and restrained, preoccupied with decoration by texture and relief rather than colour. This was particularly true of Worcester, where Thomas Bott's 'Limoges' style (he had died in 1870) was followed by experiments with decoration cut away from the surface of the vessel and with the use of coloured clays in relief as well as more orthodox pierced and relief decoration. Some of these relief and cut away vases were in the Japanese style—conscientiously correct, but distinctly ugly and dead (Fig. 44, C); others were harrowingly realistic—such as the Hadley and

Callowhill 'Potter' vases (a pair), each with a pinnacled top like a clock tower in Victorian renaissance style, the interior of the vase cut away to reveal a workshop inside which medieval potters worked, the whole modelled in the round (Fig. 44, D).

Worcester went in for elaborate essays in historic style in the eighties. An Italian renaissance nef, highly gilded and decorated in relief, was typical of their important pieces; also a careful copy of a covered vase in Louis XVI style, with gilded decoration in relief and heavily imposing. Worcester had produced vases covered with pierced decoration in the Chamberlain period of the forties; now, in the last decades of the century, a craftsman named George Owen made 're-ticulated' or pierced vases for them, each minute hole of the tracery being tooled by hand and the final result being incredibly thin-walled and delicate. These fragile vases and others with highly competent but very sentimental monochrome or blurred landscape painting on them, sometimes set off by applied ornament of tinted clay, were typical of the softening taste of the nineties (Fig. 44, E). James Hadley's 'Kate Greenaway' figures of boys and girls in regency dress, modelled in the white glazed, with touches of colour and gilt, were also typical of the revived, but sadly softened, eighteenth-century taste. The Grainger Company at Worcester also produced parian and reticulated vases with some *pâte-sur-pâte* decoration in the eighties, but in general this factory followed the Royal Worcester style and in 1889 was finally absorbed by the larger concern.

Pâte-sur-pâte as a technical innovation was really Minton's and it came from France. The constant disturbances on the continent brought many French craftsmen to England, and Marc Louis Solon was one, a refugee from the Franco-Prussian war. He had practised the *pâte-sur-pâte* technique in Paris; in England this essentially Chinese mode of decoration was used with an entirely English and Victorian effect. The embossed design was built up by applying coat after coat of slip and when dry, cutting out details with a modelling tool, the last touches being painted on with thicker slip just before firing. The result was quite unlike the oriental in spirit. Classical figures, with delicate translucent draperies, moved with a wraith-like delicacy against a dark background and on vases which followed classical Greek shapes closely: it was extraordinarily successful. Lacking the heavy pomposity of many of the porcelain styles of the seventies and eighties, the style managed also to avoid the slight silliness which seems to have crept in during the nineties, when so many other factories had decoration which was distinctly mawkish in style. *Pâte-sur-pâte* was least successful when used on the circular oriental bottle-type vases with short necks on four stumpy little feet —largely because the proportions of the vases themselves were unsuccessful.

Other late Minton wares were less attractive. Some very Frenchified vases and plates with a pedantic and frozen elegance were painted for them by A. Boullemier in the early seventies and they produced large Japanese vases with carefully painted flowers and birds that were equally chaste, but not up to the quality of the satisfying Celadon vase decorated in relief (now in the Victoria and Albert Museum) shown in the 1862 exhibition, or of the direct imitation of a white chinese vase by Leon Arnoux in the Victoria and Albert Museum, also shown in the 1862 exhibition. Their painted plates of the eighties, alas, with contemporary decoration, although of beautiful quality, are distressingly mawkish in style.

The same deterioration and failure of taste, is to be found in nearly all the porcelain of the eighties and nineties. The period of heavy pedantry and renaissance or Sèvres style (at its least attractive and most elaborate) in the seventies and eighties is followed by a frivolous and sentimental reaction, a great deal of gilt, orchidaceous flowers, misty landscapes and conventionally pretty ladies painted in too realistic a style for the medium, on vases and plates of rather mincing proportions. Two factories least affected were rather old-fashioned in their productions: Derby and Belleek. Belleek in County Fermanagh had been started by a landowner (c. 1857), John Caldwell Bloomfield, after he had noticed deposits of china clay and stone on his estate at Castle Caldwell, which he had had vetted by Kerr of the Worcester factory. The porcelain produced was hard with an attractive pearly iridescence. It was left in the white, glazed or unglazed and used for state centrepieces with sea horses, shells and other marine decoration, pierced baskets, vases and small domestic ware. Some very pretty parian type figures were also made. Perhaps because it was Irish, it had quite a genuine Georgian feeling about it, gayer and less mawkish than other late Victorian productions and much less solemn. Sea horses with shells make charming single vases (Plate 13) and some of the pieces are slightly fantastic; perhaps because Belleek was influenced for a short time in the sixties by the disastrous writhing reptiles of Palissy ware. Luckily he kept to sea animals. Thus a tea service made for Queen Victoria had a 'grounds bowl' designed in the shape of a sea-urchin, supported on branches of coral. Pierced baskets encrusted with flowers were typical and so successful that they are still made today.[1]

Derby had lived long on its eighteenth-century reputation, perhaps because it had not been prosperous. The factory had changed hands several times and there had been less opportunity for innovation. Proportion, colour, soft gilding and a sort of mellowness of style is characteristic of Derby wares to the end, because when the factory finally began to succeed (c. 1884) the advantage of the eighteenth-century tradition was at last recognized. Although, being Victorians, the new owners could not resist making improvements to the old

---

[1] Godden: *Victorian Porcelain*, p. 192.

patterns, the Crown Derby Japan ware of the late eighties and nineties is still recognizably Regency in proportion, with clean yet sturdy Grecian lines. The 'improvement' was a raised gold border to the pattern, still, thankfully in this case, discreet enough not to spoil the design. Their chief flower painter from 1882 until his death in 1888 was James Rouse. Nearly eighty when he joined them, he had been reared in an earlier tradition and his work was still fresh and good. He was succeeded by Desiré Leroy from Minton's and the coyness of his Frenchified paintings of little birds is made bearable by the sturdy proportions of the Derby vases they decorate.

Apart from parian statuary, few free standing figures were made in Victorian porcelain. There were some in the forties, but the parian replaced them and the tradition died out. Mintons made some in a bisque rather like parian and round about 1851 they produced the New Shepherd and New Shepherdess in tinted parian, eighteenth-century pastiche in style. Apart from the Derby bisque figures of 1865 already referred to and the late Worcester examples, there was little else. Copeland and Garrett made some noble reclining greyhounds, in colour, on simple squared-off moulded plinths, and several other animal figures, whilst the Rockingham factory (which only just comes into the period, having failed in 1842) made delightful barking poodles, mounted on sumptuous crimson lake or dark blue cushions with gold tassels. Rockingham also made delightful pastille-burners in the shape of cottages, castles and villas, encrusted with flowers and finished in bright clear colours and gilt. Plate 15 shows the poodle, a sheep—which might either be Rockingham or Staffordshire —and a typical castle. Many of these houses and castles were made by Staffordshire factories, although they are generally called Rockingham, and they were made in pottery as well.

But it is the pottery of the nineteenth century that is really rewarding and enjoyable, with a robust enough tradition to be able to reserve some glories for the end of the period, instead of dying away in gilded prettiness like the porcelain. In Fig. 43 I have shown typical porcelain teapot shapes, the rococo of the eighteen-forties, followed by a Worcester teapot exhibited in 1851, a Worcester 'jewelled' pot of the eighteen-sixties and a rather more ordinary bone-china pot showing both Japanese and revived eighteenth-century influence and dating from the eighteen-nineties. In Fig. 44, I show typical vase shapes of the main periods.

Victorian pottery owes its virtues to a solid Staffordshire-based tradition of manufacture and to its popular, rather than fashionable, character. Some of it can be very horrid—particularly when it tries to ape fashionable porcelain—but in every period of the reign interesting and beautiful pieces can be found. It begins with the solid Empire shapes of the Regency, slightly softened by the prevailing rococo influence.[1] The St Aubyn mug in pale blue with gilt lettering and borders was a christening mug in 1837. In Fig. 45 it stands next to mugs made c. 1860 and there has been no very great change in proportions. Plate 15 shows a commemorative plate, celebrating the birth of the Prince of Wales. The strong bold shapes of the letters of the inscription and the sharpness of the black transfer against the white letters in relief make it a very pleasing thing. The print, which looks considerably earlier than 1841, has presumably been used before, but the whole plate has the old-fashioned good manners about it which suggest an earlier date. Figure 46 shows a junket bowl of the eighteen-forties, with coloured decoration partly under and over the glaze, in pink, blue and red washes over printed outlines, in what W. B. Honey would call 'bastard famille rose'. This is in stone china, a hard, dense improved body,

---

[1] Pountney's Bristol Pottery christening and inscribed mugs ought to be mentioned here, taking on into the forties something of the old Bristol porcelain tradition; they are not in a true pottery style but they are very pretty, with highly coloured rather blowsy flowers painted in enamels and soft gilt lettering in copperplate.

Fig. 45. Group of potter mugs. Christening mug 'W. J. St Aubyn 1837', pale blue ground with gilt. Holly two-handled mug, c. 1860, transfer decoration in colour. 'Present from Exeter' mug, c. 1860, bird and nest on a bough in colour, printed with enamels added over the glaze.

Fig. 46. Junket bowl. Printed decoration with washes over the glaze 'bastard famille rose' style. Ironstone, c. 1840.

Pair of Staffordshire 'flat-back' chimney groups: *c.* 1840. (*Mrs. Spear*).

Three 'flat-back' chimney groups; the one on the left has a watch-pocket: *c.* 1860. (*Buckland Abbey*).

Staffordshire 'flat-back' group in colour: *c.* 1860. (*Buckland Abbey*).

Staffordshire beer or cider jug with decoration in relief and overglaze colour: *c.* 1860. Inscribed 'Garibaldi the Italian Patriotic Jug'. (*City Art Gallery, Plymouth*).

glazed and of greyish tone. Spode had introduced it in 1805; the famous 'Mason's Ironstone' was patented in 1813. Ironstone, made by Mason's (until bought out by Ashworth) and by Ridgways and various other firms, went on for years. By the sixties its patterns were becoming somewhat poor and stringy—particularly a rather brutal pseudo-Japanese Imari pattern.

The chintzy freshness of the ironstone designs were equalled by the simple all over transfer-printed flowers in underglaze blue by Wedgwood, Copeland (late Spode), and others. Underglaze designs were also often printed in green, purple or a sepia brown. Picturesque scenes in Italy, scenes in America, Indian hunting scenes taken from watercolours by Samuel Howitt, all appeared on dishes, sauce boats, and soup tureens. These picturesque scenes had delightful deep flower borders, also in underglaze. The designs originated in the thirties and were continued on through the next decade. A great deal of the ware was exported. Multi-coloured underglaze printing appeared in the late forties. The popular colour printed pot lids of the fifties by F. & R. Pratt of Fenton were made in this way and are avidly collected. Pratt's underglaze colour-printed domestic ware won a medal at the Great Exhibition and was exported for years afterwards to America. Its popularity is understandable, as it was made in sturdy, simple shapes decorated with *genre* scenes (like the pot lids) in reserve against a coloured ground, handles, spouts etc., left in the white and picked out in gilt; the general effect being neat and charming. The green coloured ground is a particularly attractive colour and it was plain enough never to be out of fashion.

But the winds of change did influence pottery, if more slowly than porcelain. The Wedgwood printed domestic ware of the fifties with its flowery, all-over design is more sprawly and opulent than the neat flowers of a decade before. It keeps pace with contemporary chintz designs.

G

The Gothic revival inspired Meigh and other potters to produce hard fine stone ware jugs decorated with deep cast relief decoration, often with saints under arcades of pointed arches. No doubt the shape of these, strongly vertical, with a wide upward curving lip, was thought also to be medieval. A variation on this type made as late as 1861, decorated with a sort of arcade of rustic work and plant forms, with a rustic handle of eccentric proportions, is shown in Plate 18. The textured background is typical. Other jugs decorated in relief, in stoneware or parian might have textured ground in colour. A jug in Truro Museum with a figure of a boy, birds nesting in relief on it, is in drab coloured clay against a bright blue background. The effect is fresh and charming. Just in time for 1851, Mintons produced what they called 'Majolica', a green glazed earthenware covered with plant forms in relief. Wedgwood also made this, and dessert sets both by Wedgwood and Minton and their imitators persist to the end of the era. The earlier designs—vine leaves and tendrils against a cane-work background in the same deep soft green—are the finest, the later slightly coarsened, but still attractive. The comports of the dessert services, leafy dishes on stout green stands, are amongst the most charming dishes of the nineteenth century and look especially well with fruit. Vine leaves were by no means the only design; Wedgwood did a charming sunflower-head and Mintons a chestnut dish modelled in chestnut leaves, decorated with a nut, its opened husk like a knop on the raised top. Regal pelargoniums and strawberries also appeared in the greenglaze. This nineteenth-century majolica is relatively cheap to collect and delightful in use. Like it, but comparatively evanescent in its effect, was the earthenware made by Mintons in the fifties and sixties, covered with coloured glazes known as 'caneware' and influenced in its decoration by Palissy ware, which was having a disastrous vogue in England in the sixties. These glazes, straw-coloured to deep green, were much used to set off pseudo-classical, or rather renaissance-style, figure decoration, surrounded by relief borders of renaissance detail strapwork, antique heads and so on. Some figures were made in the technique, dressed in eighteenth-century style, but for their time oddly convincing in feeling, less inspid and sentimental than Minton's own early porcelain figures and more robust than the parian.

Minton's figures remained a solitary phenomenon in mid-Victorian pottery. Figure work of their calibre did not appear again until the work of Bernard Moore, the Martin brothers and a few others in the nineties. The folk art 'flat back' figures made at the same time by various Staffordshire potters were in a rather different tradition. They sprang from the cottagey groups in the rounds which had been popular in the twenties and thirties, when highly coloured busts of John Wesley and Samuel Whitfield, biblical figures such as St Peter and St Paul in oddly flecked and sprigged robes, groups showing bull baiting, a teetotal family and so on, were made by Lakin and Poole, Obadiah Sherratt and others. The 'flat backs' were simpler and cheaper to produce and were made in many small backyard factories in Staffordshire, as well as by Sampson Smith's Longton factory, to which they are generally ascribed. They copied each other flagrantly, made short cuts by using the same mould for different figures (often with incongrous effect with suitable changes in detail), and are generally impossible to ascribe individually. They took for subject all the popular heroes of the day and of ballads and fairy stories, probably copying their portraits from cheap prints and coloured them in bright simple washes in a very shiny dark blue, orange, pink and red. Large areas were left white to show off the whiteness of the glaze and there was a discreet use of gilt to pick out telling details. Rustic backgrounds of hollow trees were generally painted inside with bright orange paint (Plate 19). The early groups are more concerned with their figures, have more colour and less white

Fig. 47. Staffordshire 'flat back' chimney clock group, c. 1860.

and gilt; the later are more concerned with novelty—they imitate the rich man's elaborate mantelpiece clock (Fig. 47) or have a watch pocket. Among the portraits, Wellington, Napoleon, the young Queen and Prince Albert, Garibaldi and Colonel Peard, his English champion, are typical. There was a terrific cult of royalty, so that the Royal children appear and royal marriages (as the children grew up) were celebrated by the appearance of a stiff ceremonial pair. There were patriotic groups—such as England linked with Turkey and France (the Crimean War). The Highlander of Fig. 48

Fig. 48. Highlander Staffordshire 'flat back' in white with touches of colour and gilt. Crimean War period, c. 1855.

links the patriotic fashion for all things Scottish[1] with the heroism and pathos of the Crimea. A Highland lass and two 'clock' groups—one with a watchpocket—appear in Plate 18. An early one is an actor—Kean perhaps—probably in Shakespearian character, making dramatic gestures from a pavilion

[1] But there was a factory making 'flat backs' in Scotland, near Prestonpans.

in very bright coloured enamels which have peeled away badly (particularly the red). In the bright colours and the dramatic gestures of the actor one sees the direct influence of the tinselled theatrical prints of the thirties and forties. Some of the most charming ' joanies ' as these flat backs were called, come from popular myth—such as the Babes in the Wood and Dick Turpin and Tom King—a favourite subject (Fig. 49). The equestrian pairs of figures were amongst the most successful. *Returning Home,* is probably the survivor of such a pair, with an unusually painted dun pony and light, bright colour

Fig. 49. Dick Turpin. One of a pair (the companion is Tom King on a white horse) Staffordshire flat back in colour, c. 1850.

(Plate 25). As well as the ubiquitous spaniels, greyhounds and dalmations were made and occasionally other breeds, although the finely modelled pug (Fig. 50) is actually modelled in the round, in naturalistic colours with a blue bow. In the 'joanie' tradition also are fancy jugs—such as Garibaldi the Italian patriotic jug (in full colour against white, mouldings picked out in dark blue, handle moulded with arms bundled together, sumounted by a helmet (Plate 20) and the pathetic little begging spaniel, crowned with vine leaves which make a rather inefficient looking lip (Plate 21).

The 'joanies' began to deteriorate in the last decades of the century, the boy and girl figures beginning to acquire an odious simpering quality. Cheap and nasty hard-paste porcelain figures from the continent were by this time disturbing their popularity. Beside their vigour, however, the higher class household wares look at the best, weakly correct. Dill-

Fig. 50. Pug. One of a pair of chimney ornaments, modelled in the round in natural colours, blue bow at neck, c. 1850.

wyn's, for example, in the sixties were producing a chaste, but rather ugly, Grecian style with transfer printed decoration and there are other misshapen pseudo-Greek pieces of the period which are rather depressing. Eastlake—after a diatribe against prevailing idiocies in ceramic taste—recommended a tea service in 'orange-porous delf' (covered internally with a glaze) and gives a cut of it: it is timidly Greek, but has pleasing plain proportions, fluted mouldings, finished off with a geometrical design in enamels and was made by Messrs Copeland. But such a ware had not sold well and was, Eastlake said, 'caviare to the multitude' although 'sound art'. Greek toilet ware by Messrs Copeland, which he also recommended, was a sad dead reproduction of its classical original. Some of the Wedgwood of the sixties, however, is interesting and its classicism anything but dead. Emile Lessore, who had worked for a short time at Minton's in 1858, was painting charming and entirely characteristic free figure subjects on the cream ware. A two-handled vase of 1862 in the Victoria and Albert Museum, on which his rather scratchily painted amorini support an inset jasper medallion of Father Time, has an engaging quality, a charm which is unusual in this slightly depressing period. A novelty which Wedgwood produced in the sixties was a rather horrid excursion into realism but might have been worse in other hands. The design was impressed in intaglio relief and flooded with translucent glaze, most often green. It gave a design in light and shade which almost seemed three dimensional, employing the same principle as the famous 'lithophanies' made at Berlin and Meissen from the eighteen-twenties onwards.

But although the higher class pottery was showing a certain nervelessness in its designs, the popular wares preserved their gaiety, especially in transfer printed commemorative designs. Early in the period there had been some excellent transfer printed railway mugs; in the sixties and seventies this tradition was carried on by the topographical souvenir mugs, not perhaps of such quality but with a certain bright charm. Even 'A Present from' mugs were very pretty as the 'Present from Exeter' with a bird on its nest in colour of Fig. 45 shows.

Freemasonry china, with all its extraordinary symbols, has a surrealist charm whilst the Ancient Order of Foresters cup and saucer of Plate 22, with a transfer print finished with a delightful deep green over the glaze, is very pretty. The decadent examples of this tradition, jubilee mugs for instance, at the very end of the century, are often more amusing than beautiful, but some of the milk jugs and beakers, with tender messages on them in a rather bad print, have an odd charm. They never were anything but cheap and may be picked up for shillings and sixpences on a junk stall, but their transfer prints are often finished with the clean bright overglaze colours and touches of cheap gilt which give them the grace of true popular art. Figure 40, along with the stone jar, shows a particularly pretty example.

But even as conventional pottery seemed at its most boring, the beginnings of a revival were discernable. Amongst William Morris's associates was the potter William de Morgan. Influenced by the Moorish or so-called Rhodian ware of the seventeenth century he used lustre once again. The simple free drawn shapes of his decoration and the soft glint of lustre against a crackle glaze background, brought an entirely new element into late nineteenth-century design. His shapes had the simplicity of the best oriental and his control of the decorative linear shapes of his designs was excellent. Whilst conventional potters were producing laboriously realistic animal paintings on porcelain vases and plates, de Morgan was designing splendid parrots, cranes and storks, conventionalized to suit his medium, but free and lively. Two examples of the tiles he designed for his Sands End Pottery at Fulham[1] are reproduced in Plate 23, carried out in tones of soft blue and purple against a fine drawn dark brown line. W. B. Honey talks of de Morgan's 'grievously imperfect technique' and Lady Sempill noted that 'his influence was limited and of short duration'. Nevertheless, he was the first of the artist potters and the best of his work is dateless in its beauty.

De Morgan was the first, but others followed. In the eighties, Doulton's of Lambeth were experimenting with stoneware and producing some hideously shaped but conscientiously decorated pseudo-Rhenish vases. Hannah Barlow's animal studies, well drawn but rather ugly, in a linear incised style, decorated some of the simpler vase shapes. George Tinworth was producing well meaning but weak realistic figures in a kind of salt glaze.

Doulton's was the springing-off ground for an entirely different type of artist potter. For the eldest of the Martin brothers, Robert Wallace, received his training at Doulton's and the Martin brothers, except in their dedication, were extremely different from de Morgan. The three Martins founded a pottery at Fulham and here they worked in salt glazed stoneware, but their work has a liveliness very different from contemporary commercial pottery. This is not to say that they were not of their time. In some ways they were remarkably late Victorian. They shared a sense of humour which was entirely contemporary—the bird tobacco jar of Plate 24 is typical of their caricature figures (often reflecting the likeness of eminent politicians) and less hideous than some of them. The 'ye thrower' figure in bluish salt glazes, is again typical of them and of its period. But their importance lies less in their figures and birds (which arouse violent feelings for or against) than in their vases, some of which have a freedom and elegance, allied to sturdiness, which is a portent of the twentieth-century artist-potter's work.

In Plate 25 are two stoneware jugs by the Martins, showing

¹ He left Morris's in 1888 and went into partnership with Halsey Ricardo at Fulham, 1888-1898.

the diverse surface textures they could produce in the stone-ware when their technique had matured. Plate 26 shows a group of their later vases, the small ones based on gourd shapes, the large vase decorated with thistle seed heads, all showing the influence of the oriental which dominated their last designs. All have very subtle and beautiful effects in the nut browns, metallic blacks and stone colours of their glazes. In colour and decoration, particularly in the scratchy linear quality of the decoration, they suggest the work of an artist in quite another technique, Arthur Rackham the illustrator.

A man whose work was complementary to the Martin Brothers, although quite unlike it in style, was Bernard Moore. His earliest work was done on his own account for Moore Brothers of Stoke-on-Trent, the family firm; later he worked as a consultant designer for Wedgwood's and other firms. As the Martins explored the possibilities of the texture of the stoneware and the shapes of their pots, so Moore worked on coloured glazes, managing to reproduce the oriental flambé and sang de boeuf glazes by the eighteen-nineties. With these he decorated little animal figures, modelled like Japanese netsuke but finished with a jewelled craftsmanship that makes them more like precious objects by Fabergé than pottery figures. But Bernard Moore in many ways is more Edwardian than Victorian.

CHAPTER VII

VICTORIAN GLASS

I USED to regard Victorian glass as a kind of poor man's Georgian. This is not so, of course. After the heavier Georgian of the forties, it developed variations of style completely its own. Like porcelain, it was particularly subject to the battle of the styles. There are in Victorian glass three distinct levels of style: the frankly opulent and expensive, generally conservative, either elaborately cut or engraved; the middle range in which most of the experiments of fashion and technique are to be found; and the folk glass of kitchen, cottage and fairground, often and even despite the inevitable cheapening at the end of the century, the most attractive of the lot. Apart from these divisions there are the novelties, the 'fancy' glass in paperweights, vases and toys, produced by the endless experiment of the industrial revolution.

The butler's pantry at Emma Place in 1841 contained quite an array of glass; '5 wine glasses, 6 ditto, 4 Tumblers, 4 Rummers, Pair Quart Decanters, Pair Pint ditto to correspond, 3 coloured Spirit bottles, with plated corks and Labels'. There was also a glass pickle bottle, sugar basin, hyacinth glass and a ground glass lampshade. All this, of course, would be basically Georgian in style but already there are important differences. The decanters, instead of the high-shouldered profile of the Regency (Fig. 51, A), have a weakly sloping curve. Their stoppers, instead of the elegant umbrella of earlier mushroom shape, are like turbans, pearshaped, more than a trifle top-heavy. The glass is deeply cut with a vertical emphasis into pillars or arches, sometimes giving a consciously gothic effect. Relatively simple examples, such as the kind one would expect to find in a middle class house like Emma Place, are pleasing and still easy to buy at a reasonable price. Elaborately cut examples are less pleasing with lumpish proportions and much sacrificed to sheer glitter (Fig. 51, B and C).

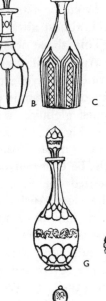

Fig. 51. Typical decanter shapes, Regency, early, mid- and late Victorian.

The Great Exhibition of 1851 saw the final elaboration of the cut-glass decanter. The advent of pressed glass, with its cheap imitation of cut-glass, had heralded a reaction against the style. Shortly afterwards engraving took the place of cutting in high fashion. The two decanters in Fig. 51, D, E shown at the Great Exhibition are so covered with cut pattern that the shape of the vessel is almost obscured. A new basic shape—one which was to be dominant for the rest of the period—has appeared, the ovoid or flattened globular decanter with long slender neck almost always finished with a scent bottle type stopper. This shape was more suited to engraving than cutting. The Apsley Pellatt group of decanters show the fashion at an intermediate stage: the first decanter is ovoid, cut and and engraved and stands upon a foot, the others are simply cut, flattened globular in shape. All have the long, gently sloping neck (Fig. 51, G, H and I).

Apsley Pellatt, however, was a most unusual and scholarly designer, and his work might be expected to be prescient of future trends. He had inherited the Falcon Glassworks in London from his father, the elder Apsley Pellatt. He had introduced into England the method of enclosing white paste ceramic portrait busts in glass (see below), which he patented in 1819. These cameos or sulphides were surrounded by simple shapes and bold, rather severe cut patterns. Apsley Pellatt the younger has been called the Wedgwood of glass making and the classical restraint of his shapes and patterns, against the over-richness of so much of the 1851 decoration, immediately tells, even in the rather unflattering cuts which illustrate the Great Exhibition Catalogue. The purity of his metal and the craftsmanship of the Falcon glass house's productions would make Pellatt glass distinguished in any period. Amongst other Victorian work, it has a spare elegance and quality which makes it the most desirable of its time. Apsley Pellatt gave up the glass house in 1852, when he became an M.P. and wished to devote himself entirely to a public life, but his brother Frederick carried on until 1895, when the firm gave up making glass and merely continued as dealers. Despite the restraint of his style, Apsley Pellatt was deeply interested in new techniques, such as the mille-fiori, of which he had seen examples on his travels, and he was particularly interested in Venetian glass.

If Pellatt's glass had an elegance influenced by continental models, the American decanter shown in 1851, had a character all its own. Independence since the Georgian period, had formed a separate style. The uncompromising shape of the Brooklyn Flint Glasswork's decanter and its straight forward all-over cutting are oddly modern in their plain boldness. After the fidgetiness of so much English work, this comes as a breath of fresh air (Fig. 51, J).

In America also by 1851 some very pleasing coloured glass had been made. Decanters in amethyst and a honey colour were made in early Victorian times by the Boston and Sand-wich Glass Company. Unhampered by excise restrictions, the glass industry could develop in a less fettered way than in Britain. Coloured glass in Britain by a combination of the vagaries of fashion and the excise, had passed its most interest-ing phase before Victoria's reign began. The great days of Nailsea and Bristol were over. However, some modest coloured glass was made, as the bottles of Emma Place with their metal wine labels, show. But it was not until after the repeal of the Excis Act in 1845, that colour began to make a comeback. By 1851, the English makers were rivalling the Bohemian in qual-ity, according to the writer of the Great Exhibition Catalogue. This meant layered colour, with opaque glass cut away to colour underneath, or colour cut away to clear glass, further embellished by gilding or painting over the glass as well. A cased or layered decanter is shown in Fig. 51, F. It has the new globular shape, and is opaque white over ruby, embel-lished on its plain, coloured base with a band of engraving. These examples are somewhat heavy in their elaboration.

But by 1851 and even more in the sixties and seventies, the battle of the styles was raging and good proportions for their own sake were not always considered. Nor fitness in decoration, for in the sixties and seventies glass followed porcelain too closely. Inspired by the Italian Renaissance, classical Greece and Rome, the engraved decoration favoured much the same models as the painted decoration on china. Upon the gently curving sides of the globular decanters there was a plethora of strap work, medallions and rather weak rococo scrolls. There was, as in china, a preoccupation with experiments in surface texture. Trailed decoration, inspired by Venetian glass, often in a colour on a plain surface, began to be used. This could be pleasing; less so were the raised blobs of coloured or opaque glass, forming roundels within elaborate strap work. There were experiments in engraving as well as the traditional method of wheel-engraving; there was acid-etching, begun as an experimental process in the thirties but now greatly developing. It was (apparently) about 1860 that the Boston and Sandwich Glass Company sent a man to Europe to learn the process and he brought back an acid-etching machine. Acid-etching was done by coating the glass with a *resist*, then cutting the pattern through it and dipping the whole in acid, which attacked the surface through the cut-away lines.

By the seventies, however, the rounded shape popular since round about 1851 had assumed its most popular variation— the 3-lipped, ovoid, footed decanter based on the proportions of a classical Greek vessel. This was a shape which lasted in fashion until the end of the century. The example shown (Fig. 51, K) was engraved with oriental dragons—the clasical and the Japanese taste united in one example. Techniques like rock crystal engraving, however, modified shape. This was a method of deep engraving, with an effect almost like carving in depth, by which the engraved lines were polished as brightly as the plain glass. This resulted in decoration

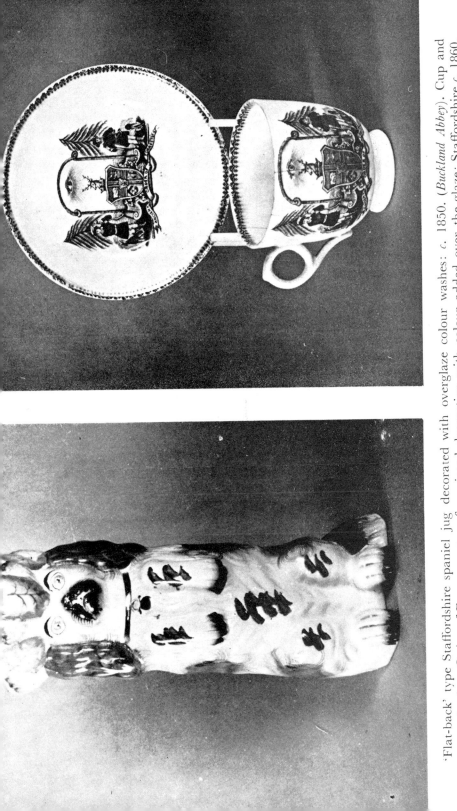

'Flat-back' type Staffordshire spaniel jug decorated with overglaze colour washes: *c.* 1850. (*Buckland Abbey*). Cup and saucer–Ancient Order of Foresters: transfer printed decoration with colour added over the glaze: Staffordshire *c.* 1860. (*City Art Gallery, Plymouth*).

Earthenware tiles by William de Morgan decorated in colour under the glaze; impressed mark 'Wm. de Morgan & Co Sands End Pottery Fulham': *c*. 1890. (*City Art Gallery, Plymouth*).

Salt-glazed stoneware by the Martin brothers of Southall; 'Ye Thrower' figure in blueish glazes *c*. 1888: tobacco jar in the form of a bird and two vases: late nineteenth century. (*City Art Gallery, Plymouth*).

imprisoned as it were in a gleaming iceberg. Unfortunately the vessels decorated by rock crystal engraving seem to have been shaped rather like lumps of melting ice. Of necessity the technique brings about a certain heaviness. 'Rock Crystal' and the new revival of 'brilliant' cut glass which occurred in the eighties and nineties produced the finest and most subtle shining effects and the most uncouth proportions. The best of the 'brilliant' glass was probably produced in America —from which its name comes—especially by the Libby Glass Company of Toledo, Ohio. The free Georgian style of the cut glass decanters of the nineties was only distantly related to true Georgian. The elaborately cut decanters stood on a duck-like spreading foot (Fig. 51, L), or were too tall and slim by Georgian standards, or were even square in section, mitre cut all over.

A few designers, influenced by William Morris and Ruskin and the ideals of the Arts & Crafts movement, were producing glass which not only brought out the beauty of the metal, but were decently proportioned as well. Such a one was Harry Powell of the firm of James Powell of the Whitefriars glass house which had made Philip Webb's table glass, commissioned by William Morris in 1859. Powell's decanter (c. 1880-1890) was after the familiar 3-lipped Greek fashion, but perfectly proportioned and decorated solely by blue glass trailing at the neck, the thin-walled purity of shape showing off the fineness of the metal (Fig. 51, M).

The new trend was most clearly to be seen in the design of drinking glasses. Philip Webb's glasses designed for William Morris in 1859, uncouth as they were, were revolutionary (Fig. 52, L). They embodied the principles of Venetian glass design which Ruskin had explained in the *Stones of Venice*, based on rapidly formed plastic shapes. The flow of their design bears this out perfectly. The goblet's doubled stem is particularly successful, it flows like water. But drinking glasses throughout the Victorian period are worth collecting,

H

showing in a small compass changes of style and also, changes in social history as the standard of living and drinking habits changed.

The period starts with glasses of a fattened-up Georgian design. But the range of shapes is increasing. In 1841 Emma Place boasted 4 rummers, 6 tumblers and no less than 3 different sets of wines. The rummers and goblets of the forties are worth acquiring, ranging as they do from elaborate engraved, cut or engraved and cut specimens to simple country bred glasses, some of them completely plain, but of a satisfyingly stout proportion, with *knopped* stem and substantial folded foot. Some noble commemorative goblets such as those in the Laing Museum, Newcastle, and the Sunderland Museum celebrating the opening of the Tyne Bridge (1831) and the Sunderland Bridge, one c. 1840 engraved with Neptune and sea horses, were produced but they are nearer Regency in style than forward looking (first goblet in procession of glasses, fig 52 A). More characteristic was the curved profile or the variations shown in the second group of glasses. The knopped stem and heavy foot, the simple vertical facets of the cutting, are typical. The wines of the period are pleasantly sturdy compared with the uneasily thin stemmed examples of the Great Exhibition. The two last examples in the group were made in coloured glass (Fig. 52, B, C, D, E).

Drinking glasses at the Great Exhibition were a riot of fancy shapes and techniques. Unfortunately, manufacturers were vying with each other to produce novelties. Of one exhibit of glass the catalogue remarked that 'the forms are borrowed from the best antiques' and this indeed was true; instead of a direct development from their own traditions, there was this restless battle of the styles. The two examples illustrated have a certain perverse charm, of the first it was remarked that it showed 'considerable novelty in design', the second, a champagne of the new hemispherical shape, was beautifully engraved with a fine and feathery vine design,

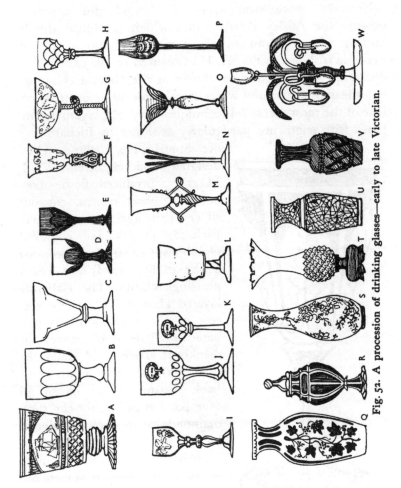

Fig. 52. A procession of drinking glasses—early to late Victorian.

but the looped stem decorated with twisted coloured threads looks uncomfortably insecure (Fig. 52, F, G).

However, more straightforward designs did appear—notably the Apsley Pellatt wines which combined simple cutting with a minimum of engraved decoration. (A cut example is shown in Fig. 52, H.) Coloured or gilt twist stems, decorating clear glass, were shown at the Great Exhibition, but the most charming wines were made of coloured glass. One of the most successful techniques was ruby-layering combined with engraving, particularly as shown by Richardson's

of Stourbridge, whose chief designer and engraver, W. J. Muckley, produced flower bouquets of great charm, cut out silvery-white against the ruby red. Richardson's cut and engraved plain glass (see vine leaf decorated goblet in Fig. 52, I) also had a pleasing solidity. The elaborate layered glass which was the success of the exhibition was perhaps a little too heavy for drinking glasses: it could be used with a ruby ground, cut back to the crystal in an all over pattern of 'richly cut sunk diamonds' as in a goblet designed by Messrs Molineaux, Webb of Manchester, but the elaborate gothic chalice-shaped goblets are something between a drinking-cup and a flower vase in size. The example illustrated in Fig. 53 is opaque white, layered back to green and finished with green

Fig. 53. Layered glass chalice-shaped goblet. Opaque white and deep green glass, with gilt and green enamels.

enamels and gilding. A charming example of plain
colour, embellished with painted gilding is the deep blue
tankard shown in Fig. 54. This, c. 1850 is by no means an
exhibition piece, but the tradition says was given by Queen
Victoria to her bedmaker as a memento. Enamels were used
also for the decoration of the goblets and carafes or jugs of
drinking sets, with charming flower painting very much in
the style current on china. Water goblets would be decorated
with sea weeds, water lilies or iris—so that the subject of the
decoration was suitable even if the technique was hardly
appropriate to glass.

After the exuberance of the Great Exhibition, later Victorian drinking glasses seem a little tame. The Venetian style
had been foreshadowed in 1851; by 1870, rather better understood, it was the prevailing influence and the prettiest glasses
of the seventies were made with delicate twisting stems and
applied trailing (Fig. 52, M). It looked, and was, fragile. Only
in Philip Webb's design of 1859 were its principles under-

Fig. 54. Tankard. In deep blue glass
with gilded inscription 'Remember
Me' and formal swag and sprigs
c. 1850. Said to have been a gift from
Queen Victoria.

stood and employed in a truly new and creative way. Goblets often very delicately engraved were subtly wrong in proportion, so that they looked unwieldy. A rummer and wine, from the Levant Mine, St Just, Cornwall (Fig. 52, J, K), and dating from the second half of the century show the better type of vernacular glass, heavy but not unpleasing with their simple cutting and etched inscription. As far as fashion was concerned, cutting was out and the rock crystal technique produced some pinched and disagreeable shapes. Simple coloured wines and claret tankards made for the middle class market are pleasing but coloured glass—which could be obtained in various tones of ruby, bright green, emerald and light peacock green, dark purple and canary—decorated with painted gilt and engraving could result in an object which looked highly costly, but ugly. As the century advanced, decoration became more academically exact and period, but also more dead. At the same time the Morris inspired handful of designers were producing new shapes in drinking glasses. Harry Powell's wine glasses were more revolutionary looking than his decanter. The last group of wines in Fig. 52 shows the free flowing shapes of glass designed by Harry Powell at the end of the century. The first is clear glass with applied green decoration (52, N), the second and third tinted with trailed decoration (52, O, P). This faint decoration, like ripples on a pool, and the plain but extravagant proportions of the last two glasses, suggest the 'fin de siecle' world of Beardsley decoration and art nouveau. They would equally suit the austerity of a Mackintosh or Voysey interior. The sensibility shown in these designs of the inherent decorative quality of the glass itself, their simplicity and restraint, presage some of the best modern design. Meanwhile the 'old legitimate' trade of cut glass having revived, reproduction Georgian wines were making an appearance. A free adaptation of the old balusters, with added fluting on the lower half of the bowl was pleasing. The unrestrained brilliance of diamond cutting, added to acid etching, produced some rather fussy glasses of high quality craftsmanship.

In the middle class house of the eighteen-forties, such as Emma Place, there was little room for elaborate ornamental glass. The drawing-room boasted a 'Pair of ground and cut glass flower stands', but all the other glass had a useful function. It was at the Great Exhibition that the glass manufacturers really let their imaginations go, producing vases and ornamental glass of enormous elaboration. This was principally carried out in cased or layered glass, often with painted decoration in enamels. Some very complicated cut glass patterns, mostly on vases shaped like a classical urn, also appeared, and engraved figure subjects, which, on vases shaped like Greek vessels, got the most rave notices in the Art Journal Catalogue. These have the virtue of good proportions and superb craftsmanship, producing a sort of cold marmoreal perfection. The layered glass, although sometimes faintly ridiculous in the eccentricity of its towering shapes, was frankly gay in colour, not only with opaque overlay cutting through to colour, but with metallic grounds, like those produced by 'Mr Mellish of London', after 'Mr Hale Thompson's process', by which the vases were made with 'double sides', the silver precipitated between (Fig. 52, Q, vase with vine decoration). Rice Harris of Birmingham produced some of the most elaborate cased vases, most of them decorated with vaguely gothic motifs carried out by means of cutting, engraving and gilding on shapes which were an extraordinary mixture of classical and free-style medieval. One vase was black coated, with white enamel, richly cut and ornamented with gold and silver; another was opaque yellow, cut and scalloped with gilt chased flowers; the prettiest and most simple was ruby, with cut and gilded lines (Fig. 52, R). A vase of dark opaque blue, cut and scalloped and ornamented with leaves and acorns in silver looks most attractive.

One of the immediate results of the Great Exhibition was

the making of chimney-piece lustres. These were shown by
Count Harrach of Bohemia in 1851, much admired and
immediately became the fashion. These lustres, consisting of
a cup-shaped vase upon a high stem and solid circular foot
in opaline finished with gilt scrolls, had cut glass prismatic
pendants dangling from them, which tinkled agreeably whenever a draught set them moving. Mostly with gilded decoration, they come in rather insipid drawing-room colours, a
pink rather like milk jelly, a pale emerald. In a good strong
colour they can be highly attractive. This type may not have
been in high fashion for long, but as a conceit for suburban
villa drawing-rooms, lasted nearly to the end of the century.

The layered vases have an engaging vulgarity; the lustres
also, with a chime like tinkling earrings. The painted vases,
generally with opaque grounds, enamelled with chaste flower
bouquets, were in a purer taste but were so like their porcelain counterparts as to be hardly worth the trouble. They
are, if anything, better proportioned than many of the china
vases of the same vintage. Figure 52, S shows one by Richard-
sons of Stourbridge decorated by W. J. Muckley. Although
painted flower decoration was the most common, figure subjects and idyllic scenes, some in sepia monochrome, also
appeared. Most effective on the white also were simple gilt
rococo flourishes, finished with plain gilt bands at neck and
foot. Some transfer-printed decoration, often with added gilt,
was used, the least effective perhaps being the rather weedy
classical figure subjects in black. These decorated opalines
were on white or greyish white opaque glass backgrounds.
But opaque or opaline glass plain or finished with gilt borders
could be in a large range of colours. Most of the jewel colours
—amber, opal, turquoise, topaz, chrysoprase, ruby etc.—were
made, also various shades of red, blue and green, even a
black. Sometimes a vase was made in two colours; white with
a green base, for example, with a suggestion of a flower rising
from its calyx; sometimes the texture of the glass was delib-

erately roughened to give an added value to the additional colour. A favourite motif was a dark blue or green opaline snake modelled gripping the sides or stem of the vessel. The shapes of coloured opaline glass (see typical vase in Fig. 52, I) were only very distantly based on the classical. However, imitation Greek vases were made in the black by Christy of Lambeth (c. 1849). These had painted red figure subjects on them in a very fair imitation of the style and their proportions, save for a slightly uncivilized moulding just above the foot, were good.

The classical taste was to be one of the prevailing modes in the vases of the sixties and seventies, in fact it remained an important element in vase design to the end of the century. The Victorians' classical education had given them a deep respect for the Greeks and Romans.

In their show pieces, such as glass vases tended to be, they used this important ceremonial style. The 'Elgin' vase by John Northwood (now in the City Art Gallery, Birmingham), modelled on a red figure amphora, is 15½ ins high and has the mounted figures from the Parthenon carved in relief upon it by the cameo process, by which an upper layer of white opaque glass is cut away to expose dark glass below, only in this case clear upon clear glass was used. Intricate bands of patterning—such as the palmette and Greek key design—are etched. The whole looks like a ghost of a Greek vase. This was finished in 1873. Cameo glass proper developed a little later and the style (at its height in the eighties) spans a period from c. 1876 to the nineties. This was a purely decorative technique by which neo-classical figure groups in white relief were set off by the background of dark glass to which the vases or plaques were cut back. It was a most lengthy and costly process—an attempt to emulate the Portland vase in Victorian terms—and examples of it have always been rare and costly and realize large sums at auction today. It is analogous in style to the *pâte-sur-pâte* of porcelain, being made at the same time, though much more expensive.

The vases have elegant and restrained shapes, beautifully balanced, although after the manner of very late Romanized Greek, but the florid figure work is insipid and in the later work rather vulgarly *luxe* and sometimes faintly salacious. The last remains of the classical style were to be found in the experiments in texture, with crackled, streaked glass (moss agate) made by Stevens & Williams at Brierly Hill, in Scotland by James Couper & Sons of Glasgow ('Clutha' glass designed by Christopher Dresser). These, shaped like amphorae and relying for their effect solely on proportion and texture, were nearer classical in feeling than any of the earlier laborious imitations.

The word 'Venetian' had been used in the Great Exhibition to describe styles that were at best a very free English interpretation. Apsley Pellatt, who had actually studied Venetian techniques, did show glass of a Venetian technique interpreted in English styles. This was frosted or 'ice-glass'. Messrs Bacchus of Birmingham exhibited a vase in this style at the Great Exhibition (Fig. 52, U). But just as table glass in the sixties and seventies copied seventeenth-century Venetian detail, so did the decorative glass. In the sixties the vases have a fine-blown globular body and are elaborately wheel-engraved with renaissance motifs, the designs being oddly static and formal. The (twisted or ribbed) handles alone are lively, with a flowing quality. A little later, vases with covers with finials like steeples, ribbed double handles, raised trailing like the spines of dragons and applied decoration appeared. Those made in Birmingham (c. 1875) are nearer the seventeenth-century Venetian in spirit. They were made in clear glass. Their slightly fantastic shapes were carried a step further in the flower stands, which became fashionable at about the same time. These had a central cup or trumpet shaped vase on a long stem rising above three or four hanging baskets. The baskets hung from elaborate twists, or some-

times from fern leaves. The fern leaves and baskets themselves were often decorated by coloured trailing, ruby, green
or blue (Fig. 52, W). The earlier examples were simpler, often
in clear glass, but in the later centre pieces, often mounted
on a mirror base or plateau, fantasy ran riot. The Venetian
influence became very remote. This was true of all the vases
of the latest years of the century.

The glass historians censure of the 'Victorian manufac-
turer in love with his own dexterity',[1] is unhappily true of
this period. The flower stands and centre pieces died out in
a mass of coloured or coloured and plain fidgety confections;
baskets with waved edges adorned with applied twists hanging
from corkscrew supports, the central vase spiky with crimp-
ing. Occasionally the rustic ones, delicately blown tree trunks
with accompanying flower holders, have a certain *fin de siècle*
charm.

As far as decorative glass was concerned, the last years of
century died out in a confusion of novelty styles and techniques. A free oriental style used Japanese motifs to decorate
vases made of the double layered 'satin glass', a complicated
process, following novelty for its own sake, which the real
Japanese craftsman would probably have considered debased.
Satin glass used an opaque glass base, moulded with channels
to form an air twist beneath a coloured clear outer layer.
Sometimes an additional opaque outer layer was used to etch
away, leaving the decoration in relief. Acid was used to give
the slightly matt 'satin' finish. Sometimes satin glass followed
no known style; the most fantastic free crimped and pinched
shapes were used to show it off, vases being made in bowl
shapes, often with crumpled sides, sometimes oddly vegetable
in form, generally mounted on rusticated feet. A very popular
pattern, both here and in America, was the diamond-moulded
underlay of opaque glass, beneath an outer layer of colour.
This gave a shadowy diamond pattern all over the vessel, a

[1] W. A. Thorpe: *History of English & Irish Glass*; Vol. 1, p. 290.

little like fish scales. One of the novelty techniques, the so-called 'Burmese' glass, originated in America. This was an opaque glass, first made by the Mount Washington Glass Co. of New Bedford, Mass., greenish yellow, shaded under heat treatment to a deep pink. Iridescent glass also was extremely popular—notably Thomas Webb's 'Bronze' (shown at the Paris Exhibition of 1878). Webb's also made the Burmese glass. Tinted opalescent glass, decorated with a deposit of silver on its surface, which was then engraved, also popular.

So much for the vases. The comports or centre pieces followed much the same lines of development, centre pieces tending to be replaced by flower-stands in the last years. Claret-jugs likewise followed the same evolution as decanters. They were amongst the most successful shapes of the classical style.

Water jugs, however, being more utilitarian, followed a slightly different course. The painted or engraved clear glass jugs of the fifties had followed the shapes of Greek pottery, the ovoid footed shape of the Venetian influence had come next, often with ribbed handle and engraved and applied decoration, but in the sixties the tankard shaped jug had become popular and this, often decorated with delightfully engraved cool looking nauralistic fern patterns, remained in fashion until the end of the century. Amongst the cheaper glass—notably amongst the cheap ruby—a short-necked, pitcher-shaped jug was also popular from the sixties and Sowerbys of Gateshead also produced a delightful pitcher-shaped jug which derived from the eighteenth-century tradition in its proportions.

It is in the glass devised for the market-stall that some of the most charming Victorian glass is to be found, both English and American. As far as the English glass was concerned, the vernacular tradition in design was conservative, utilitarian, with a fondness for colour whenever possible—probably because the metal of the cheap plain glass had no great virtue on its own. Shapes were sensible, deriving from late eighteenth-century or regency models rather than from the eccentricities of Victorian fashionable taste. The American tradition was slightly different, firmly based on Georgian, but having developed its own local variations in technique and patterns, it was less conservative. Indeed, America really first developed the technique of pressing glass between a mould and a plunger and American pressed glass was more ingenious and interesting in its design than the early English.

American designs were even imported into England. The early American glass of the thirties was decorated with 'lacy' patterns, relief decoration surrounded by a finely stippled or matted ground. The early English pressed work that has survived merely imitated the cut glass patterns of the time, which tended to be too heavy for the technique to reproduce entirely happily. However, such small articles as cream jugs (Fig. 55) or little plates, jam dishes and sugar basins have a certain country freshness about them. They, and the tumblers produced at the same time, are truly poor man's Georgian. A pressed glass creamer of 1899 (when the revival of the

Fig. 55. Pressed glass cream jug.
In imitation of cut glass. c. 1840.

fashion for cut glass had brought about the imitation of cut glass once again) is not quite as nicely proportioned, its pattern a little too complicated and fussy, but it shows nevertheless how the Georgian tradition had persisted.

The Georgian tradition in American glass design was a jumping-off point for their pressed glass design. The early designs were not imitations, although based on late Georgian principles. The 'lacy' designs were perfectly suited to the technique, and American 'cup plates' as made by the Boston and Sandwich Glass Company (1825-1888, pressed glass until 1860) are well worth collecting. There were some splendid ships—notably the *Benjamin Franklin*—a paddle steamer with a border with anchors, starfish and a patriotic eagle with wings outspread in relief against a raised pebbly background. A square dish celebrating the U.S. Frigate *Constitution* in full sail with a 'matted' background to a border of hearts and five pointed stars, the whole finished with a scalloped edge, is another beauty. These raised designs are sturdy and attractive: portraits of presidents, war heroes, railroad engines, such topicalities as the Tippecanoe Hard Cider Campaign (expressed by a picture of a log cabin and a barrel) each with an inscription in relief in fat-face capitals, all as perfectly suited to the character of the technique as the woodcuts were related to the chap-book printing earlier in the century. These 'lacy' pressed glass designs are in the best tradition of popular art. They were made until the eighteen-fifties. The Sandwich Company also made candlesticks, salts, scent bottles, decanters, sugar bowls, comports, vases and lamps in plain, coloured and opaline glass. They also made peculiar little joke pieces in the form of upturned top-hats which are highly regarded and collected today, although they are novel rather than ornamental. Their single candlesticks are particularly attractive—especially the dolphin design. The same dolphin was also used as a support for a small comport. A comport in opaque white or a plump shape with a discreet pressed pattern, at the Metropolitan Museum of Art, New York, is particularly good, also a vigorous white jug with a medallion of a ship in full sail pressed on the side, raised narrow fluting at the base and a rather nautical looking rope-like double border at its rim. With a few exceptions, all the Sandwich shapes were good. It was only in the last years of the factory, when the emphasis was turning to cut rather than pressed glass, that shapes became fussy and over complicated. Another good American factory specializing in pressed glass was at Pittsburg, where the sand is especially good for glass making and there were several glasshouses. This was the James B. Lyon Company of the O'Hara Glass Works, who in 1867 showed pressed glass at the Paris Exposition and took a first prize.

English pressed glass was slow to develop its own particular style. A style comparable to the American 'lacy' style with its rounded raised patterns appeared late. By the sixties the possibilties of areas of roughened glass to set off the pressed pattern were being explored. A standing dish in Mr Hugh Wakefield's collection, decorated with vertical bands of alternate pressed and roughened glass from a scalloped edge has a charming regency striped effect, very simple and decently proportioned. In the seventies and eighties something like the American 'lacy' style was being used on commemorative dishes, sugar bowls and the like. An amber Jubilee dish in the Plymouth Museum is typical (Plate 27), and the hob-nailed effect of the dotted pattern has a vigour quite unlike the etiolated elegance and novelty for its own sake fashionable in expensive fancy glass. But the craze for novelty did in the end destroy the naïve charm of pressed glass.

The first novelties of the seventies were amusing enough —two hands cupped together to form a bowl, finished with a fantastic cuff of vine leaves and grapes, the whole satin-finished. Or a dish with pierced borders like an openwork basket, the centre filled with a naturalistic design of grapes and leaves. Pressed baskets of fruit in deep green bottle glass in pairs as fireplace ornaments also have a rich and full blown charm. There was some charming opaque domestic ware—an example being the cream jug of Plate 28. The firm of Sowerby's at Gateshead produced dishes and comports in a pressed basket-work design, often with deep pierced borders. These, in turquoise or opal opaque glass, are fresh and pretty. A classical vase in jet has decent proportions (Fig. 52, V) but funereal colour, but the odd shaped novelty vases and plant-pots which Sowerby's also produced show novelty run mad. A spill vase in jet, with gilt figures of Jack & Jill in relief (Kate Greenaway period dress) is a squared-off bucket shape with slightly concave sides, on a moulded plinth which looks like brickwork. The taste for the Japanese style had a disastrous effect. Sowerby's and others produced vases and bowls of eccentric shape in extraordinary splashed and mottled effects, in which the elaboration of the mottling fought with the mouldings of the pressed glass.

Often square-shaped vases stand on four feet; one ill-proportioned brute with a crenellated rim ending in irregular fangs has a fluted shaft at each corner ending in a claw foot; an odd boat-shaped vase ends in a swan, the base of which makes a foot, with two other plain supports.

Even at the end of the nineteenth century, however, delightful things like glass marbles were being produced, in a style completely unspoiled by commercialization. These marbles were decorated with coloured enamel twist, the very small ones for solitaire. They were made of a greenish glass. Made by the local bottle glass-houses of deep green glass were the door-stops and paper-weights made throughout the period. The door-stops are ovoid, on heavy flat bases, up to 5 or 6 lbs in weight and decorated with bubbles formed by denting the glass when hot and gathering fresh glass over it, the minute air pockets making the bubbled effect. The bottle green paper-weights are deeper, some nearer ovoid than

Two salt-glazed stoneware jugs by the Martin brothers: *c*. 1898. (*City Art Gallery, Plymouth*).

Salt-glazed stoneware by the Martin brothers: *c*. 1899-1900. (*City Art Gallery, Plymouth*).

Jubilee commemoration dish in amber pressed glass: 1887.
(*City Art Gallery, Plymouth*).

Cream jug in white opaline pressed glass: *c*. 1860. (*Buckland Abbey*).

circular, than the usual millefiori paper-weight.[1] Imprisoned inside them are ghostly white flowers, made by chalk sprinkled on the marver with the design on it, soft glass being gathered on to it, followed by another gathering immediately to enclose the whole design. Like the heavy glass mushrooms—which are linen-smoothers—most local glasshouses made the weights and stops. They made them until handmade bottling came to an end, so that they are difficult to date precisely. Other locally made things, which kept to their traditional shapes over a long period were the pickle jars and bottles (the Americans produced very fine moulded bottles with decorations and inscriptions early in the period) and the hyacinth glasses. Emma Place boasted a hyacinth glass in the drawing-room and a pickle jar in the butler's pantry. Hyacinth glasses, in smoky purple or green or blue, although of rough glass, look very decorative with a hyacinth growing in them. They are still cheap and fairly easily come by. These, and pickle jars and pretty straight-sided sweet jars with hat-like lids, sometimes turn up on market-stalls and in junk shops.

[1] See Bric-à-Brac section at end of next chapter.

I

CHAPTER VIII

SILVER AND PLATE, JEWELLERY
AND BRIC-À-BRAC

In 1878 Sir Charles Lock Eastlake could write: 'In the whole range of art-manufacture there are no more deplorable examples of taste than the silver side-dishes, soup tureens, cruet-stands and candlesticks of the nineteenth century. The most extravagant forms are enriched with ornament which is either a caricature of Renaissance detail, or simply feeble representations of natural form.' His indignation dealt perhaps too savagely with a period which did produce a few examples of charming plate. But on the whole Victorian silver is the least attractive form of Victoriana. Only those with an intense nostalgia for the whole period could feel an enthusiasm for the full range of its silver design. Because of its ostentatious nature silver and plate probably suffered the worse faults of Victorian design. It was ideal for official presentations and for show. In the smallest pieces, where no account of display need be taken, it could sometimes be charming.

The period began with a mass of technical innovations. Britannia metal, a soft alloy made of tin, antimony and copper, had been invented shortly before Victória's reign. In 1840 Elkington's of Birmingham patented electroplating. This revolutionized the Birmingham silversmiths' work and brought in a time of constant improvement in plating. By 1855, it had also brought about the decay of the Sheffield plate industry. From 1820 the use of steam power had mechanized some of the processes of silversmithing—teapots, cream

130

jugs and shallow vases could now be 'spun' into shape.
Throughout the period the production of silver and plate
became more and more commercialized, so that at the end
there was that dichotomy between 'trade' silver and crafts-
man-designed work which exists today.

When the house at Emma Place was sold in 1841, no plate
appears in the catalogue, save a 'Brass Table Kettle and
Stand' in the butler's pantry and a 'Metal Tea Pot and Soup
Ladle' in the kitchen! No doubt the silver was sold separately.
The 'Metal Tea Pot and Ladle' were probably Britannia
metal. This, although it has a very penny-plain appearance,
somewhere between silver and pewter, was often pleasingly
designed. A tea-pot and cream jug of 1840 by Joseph Wolstenholme of Sheffield in the Sheffield City Museum has a simple
proportion not unlike late eighteenth-century stoneware
designed in the Grecian taste. The sensible lines of both vessels
have the look of being designed for use that the best Victorian engineering has. Wolstenholme's significantly, was the
firm which commissioned Alfred Stevens, one of the first Victorian designers, to design a set of 'hunting knives' for the
Great Exhibition in 1851.

If only Victorian plate could have been designed at such
a functional level! But if by the thirties the clean neo-Greek
lines of Regency silver were being cluttered up by an inva-
sion of rococo ornament, by the forties several different styles
had complicated design further. The most popular style was
the rococo, but there was also rococo with naturalistic
ornament, the medieval or Gothic style, and deliberate copies
of classical Greek and Roman designs, produced by foreign
experts for electrotyping. In 1846 Sir Henry Cole, calling
himself Felix Summerly, had won a first prize from the Royal
Society of Arts for a design for a tea set carried out by
Mintons. The cream jug was also produced in silver and glass.
His success gave Sir Henry the idea of beginning Summerly's
Art Manufactures, a scheme by which eminent artists were to

design for industry. Sir Henry deplored naturalistic ornament. 'Decoration should consist of appropriate motifs drawn from nature and relating to the use of the article'. He overlooked the fact that his artists had no knowledge of the techniques they were designing for and he obviously had little sense of his material, since his pottery design was considered equally suitable for porcelain, silver and glass. His idea of appropriate symbolic decoration led back to naturalism in the end. Nevertheless, the Summerly Art Manufactures did eschew the worst elaborations of rococo and the 'symbolic ornament' could have a certain charm, as in the guardian angels of the christening mug designed in 1849 by Richard Redgrave and exhibited by S. H. & D. Gass in 1851. This mug was re-issued in 1865-6. A design similarly symbolic is to be seen in the flagon presented by Plymouth Corporation to their Mayor, Charles Norrington on the birth of his son in 1863. This has a muddled design, redeemed by the charm of its detail. Here, naturalistic, symbolic raised figure decoration is super-imposed on a shape based on seventeenth century continental work, which is also plentifully decorated with period strapwork and scrolls. (Plate 29)

Victorian silver is difficult to date stylistically because of this muddled attitude. One might say that the forties mostly produced rococo, with and without naturalistic decoration, Gothic work or direct classical reproductions and that the period of the Great Exhibition complicated matters, introducing many more variations on these three main styles. But despite the search for novelty many of the designs shown at the Great Exhibition had first appeared in the forties and there is little difference between the periods, save that the earlier the piece, the more charming, is generally the rule. Early Victorian rococo tea services have a plump charm that makes them well worth acquiring. The lobed pumpkin shape of the service illustrated (Plate 30) by Joshua Savery of London, 1842, is very pretty and the naturalistic sprigs on the lids of both tea and coffee pot finish the pieces off in a most satisfying way. A waisted, high tea kettle shape, also lobed, could be effective. This and a shape like that of the mid-eighteenth-century tea caddy often stood upon scroll feet. There was also a very solid pear-shaped pot, generally on four feet, rather too portly to be attractive. These might be engraved and embossed with flowers and acanthus leaves, given spouts in the form of dragons engraved with Elizabethan strapwork decoration and finished off with figures of chinamen sitting on their lids (as in one so-called 'Elizabethan' style service). They might even be decorated by figure subjects in relief, which gave a rather lumpy effect, obscuring the basic shape. Even so, naturalism rarely got out of control. There is still a pleasing air of fantasy about the early rococo. By the time of the Great Exhibition, however, despite Sir Henry Cole's plea, naturalism was definitely beginning to get out of control, and although 'appropriate motifs drawn from nature' might be cited for the cream ladle in the shape of a buttercup, teapots made entirely from leaf forms or in the shape of a pitcher plant, or of Sir Joseph Paxton's Victoria regia waterlily, were more ingenious than beautiful. On a small scale, even out and out naturalism could be charming. The cream ladles and caddy spoons are engaging trifles. Leaves, with a twisted stalk for handle were favourite shapes for caddy spoons. The vine leaf and bunch of grapes was a favourite. Other leaves, flowers, even (a surrealist touch) a little open hand, were made.

But naturalism on a large scale could be disastrous. Huge presentation pieces in style like the Albert Memorial; the centre piece or wine-fountain obscured by its surrounding modelled symbolic figures, tamed lions and prancing horses, presented a spiky, realistic and weighty appearance. Far too large except as centre pieces in Victorian baronial halls, they can scarcely be lamented. Again, on a small scale, such realistic modelling can be pleasing.

By the fifties the rococo style had its own sub-divisions—

Renaissance, Arabesque, Venetian, even Egyptian—although
the Egyptian motifs seem to have been a hang-over from the
Regency. Books describing famous continental masterpieces of
the past, with wood engraved illustrations were becoming
available. The *Illustrated Hand-book of the Arts of the Middle
Ages* translated from Labarthe (John Murray, 1855, incidentally with a handsome acknowledgement to Apsley Pellatt
for providing subjects for illustrations) and Owen Jones's
work on the Alhambra, came out in the forties. The ornament illustrated, and more or less free interpretations of the
shapes as well, were carried out to satisfy this antiquarian
taste. Thus the Cellini style gave rise to extraordinarily complicated thin necked ewers, elongated jugs and coffee pots,
with embossed or engraved figure groups. Occasionally, however, the antiquarians were served by a good designer who
had a natural affinity for the particular period style in which
he worked and whose flair could make of it a re-interpretation.
Several French designers (the French revolution of 1848 had
brought them over) were working for Birmingham firms. One
of the finest was Pierre-Emile Jeannest whose jug, designed
in 1853 with an all over decoration of amorini and vines, is
a noble creation, expressing the vigour and abundance of mid-
Victorian civilization in the amplitude of its proportions and
decoration, but perfectly controlled and satisfying in shape.
The quality of Jeannest's work lies in its professionalism—it
lacks the feeling of amateur experiment, of incomplete understanding which marred so many English antiquarian pieces.
An Englishman who was a complete professional, however,
was Alfred Stevens, a sculptor who had spent eight years
training in Florence. He had been reared at Blandford in
Dorset with the sturdy buildings of English Renaissance all
round him and he had a natural understanding of the high
Renaissance and a fastidious sense of proportion in ornament.
Throughout the fifties he sent models of his designs to
Thomas Bradbury and Sons of Sheffield, which were carried

out in silver, electro- and nickel-plate, only one of which—
a tray in the Victoria and Albert Museum—survives.

Alfred Stevens had an unusually complete knowledge of
the process of silversmithing, unlike the Academicians
designing for the Summerly Art Manufactures. At least one
of the practitioners of Gothic design was similarly trained.
Augustus Welby Pugin was an architect and reformer with
a burning sense of the beastliness of his own time and the
grace of medieval civilization. A convinced Roman Catholic,
he brought a seriousness to all he did. His Gothic designs in
silver, as in furniture, show a careful use of gothic motif and
architectural detail to translate the Gothic spirit into the
terms of his own time. John Hardman of Birmingham, for
whose firm he designed the Gothic teapot in the Victoria
and Albert Museum, was also a Roman Catholic and fully
shared his ideals. Pugin's work in metal links up with the
work of the Pre-Raphaelite designers and architects, like
G. E. Street, in other spheres. Street was one of the enlightened architects who superintended every minute detail of a
building he was working upon. He had a fair idea of what
he wanted, for example, in the way of church plate. A chalice
by Keith, a London maker of 1849 at St. Mary's Par, one of
Street's first church designs—is significantly plain and beautifully proportioned and completely medieval in feeling. This
undercurrent of sound design in the Gothic style can be found
pretty well throughout the period, especially in church plate,
which even in the designs submitted to the Great Exhibition,
preserved a certain correctness of proportion. Thus in 1866,
a sidelight is thrown upon the production of church plate in
Gerard Manley Hopkins's letters to Robert Bridges, when he
negotiates through G. E. Street with Keith for a cruet. The
silver top he designs himself (he encloses sketches of a simple
Gothic design for Bridges to see); the glass vessel has to be
specially blown for him. The whole was to have cost about
two pounds. This direct dealing between patron and maker,

the old tradition of bespoke craftsmanship, is responsible for much quietly good work, which persisted despite the vagaries of fashion.

Victorian classical like the Gothic, was a serious style. As in glass, it was most fashionable in the decade after the Great Exhibition. The classical and Renaissance, especially Venetian, style was in the ascendant in the sixties and seventies. A Greek style, mostly directly derived from Greek vase shapes, with a disciplined restraint that resulted in a style not unlike a heavier Adam, was popular in the eighteen-sixties. The good simplicity of its proportion probably owed a great deal to the innate conservatism of the silversmiths. Such firms as Barnard, Garrard and Hennell in London (each with a long eighteenth-century tradition) produced excellent, if slightly heavy, dinner services in this style. Fig. 56, A, B shows pieces from a provincial tea and coffee service in a style based on the plain Grecian shape, probably given as a coursing prize, greyhounds decorating the lids. Although slightly awkward in shape, it has a strait-laced charm.

By the eighteen-seventies, however, silver design in general had become very dreary. The chief silversmiths were making work that was at its best only in imitation of other styles, while provincial work was gawky and ill-proportioned, stringy in its detail, overladen with strap work and beading and meaningless engraved flourishes. As Eastlake observed, 'a large proportion of modern plate is stamped in patterns which have no more artistic quality than the ornaments of a wedding cake'. 'Compare them with the charming examples of antique silver which may still be seen in the windows of a curiosity shop,' he says 'and 'observe how much we retrograded in this department of manufacture.' Gradually indeed a reaction did set in. There was a general agreement with Eastlake about the superiority of eighteenth-century design and a certain frilly Adam reproduction style became fashionable. This has a pinched quality immediately recognizable

Fig. 56. Typical silver shapes A. B, late 1850's-60's C, 1890's.
D, 1880's (by Christopher Dresser).

from earlier Victorian reversions to the eighteenth century,
for it is light and flimsy, and makes a great deal of Adam
husk decoration and the outside trappings of the style. A
plated teapot of a pattern current in the last years of Victoria's reign is illustrated in Fig. 56, C. A subtle stringiness of
detail, a certain vulgarization of line and proportion would

make this teapot immediately distinct from real eighteenth-century work. Nevertheless, this reproduction Georgian is reasonable to buy and easy to live with, light and unostentatious and is even, by now, beginning to gather a certain nostalgic period feeling of its own. It is silver with a Kate Greenaway charm.

A more valuable reaction to commercialized design was that shown by the Arts and Craft Guild of which William Morris was a Master, although he himself never designed plate. Stimulated by what Mr Gerald Taylor has described as 'a strange mixture of Japanese and medieval' these designers, working as the furniture-makers and artist potters did in small craft-workshops, gradually evolved a new style. Their artistic pedigree of integrity of design and craftsmanship can be traced back to the ideals of such as Pugin, Hardman and G. E. Street. Their pieces were decorated by embossing and casting, by enamels, mother of pearl and stones set *en cabochon*. Charles Robert Ashbee (1863-1942), W. A. S. Benson (1854-1924) and Oscar Ramsden (1873-1939) were three of the leading craftsmen. The style, which had a certain conscious uncouthness about it was shown at its most typical in the large beaten silver chargers and dishes with a deep border of embossed ornament; flowing arabesques based on Renaissance patterns, formalized plant-form derived from William Morris or the abstract shapes of Celtic ornament. The asymmetrical forms of Celtic ornament, the trumpet-shaped curves and flowing linear quality led surely to *art nouveau* and the beginnings of the modern movement. Charles Robert Ashbee, who set up a workshop at Essex House as well as a printing press, also designed jewellery. In this the style was seen at its best. There were two great weaknesses in the movement, the first that it tended to encourage a certain amateurishness and arty-craftiness, the second that, as Eastlake complained, it cost so much more to buy than the ordinary commercial production.

Gertrude Jekyll's work in silver was the best kind of amateurishness. Her description of the workshop at Munstead Wood, with its loving appreciation of tools and materials, and the many pieces gathered there as inspiration for her work, shows a healthy wind of change blowing through cultured taste. Her own designs might be lacking originality, but at least they were well-mannered and proportioned and her sensible remarks in such a book as *Home and Garden*, which was widely read, had a great influence on the mildly cultivated upper middle class.

In the work of a designer like Christopher Dresser (d. 1904) the emphasis was on the Japanese side of the 'strange mixture'. Christopher Dresser was trained under Henry Cole and at the Government School of Design in London during the forties and fifties. He followed Richard Redgrave as lecturer in botany at the London School and this training in the understanding of natural form is obvious in the uncluttered, one might almost say organic, lines of his own designs. In reaction to the clutter around him in English contemporary design he conceived an enthusiasm for Japanese art, collected it himself and, in 1867, managed to make a visit to Japan. The interesting thing about Dresser is that, first and foremost, he was a professional industrial designer, never an arts and crafts man. All his designs were carried out with an engineer's precision and knowledge of industrial processes and with an economy of material which he hoped would keep them within the reach of those of moderate means. They were extremely plain and unlike the *japonaiserie* of the glass makers and potters, were not so concerned with Japanese decorative conceits as with the oriental principles of proportion and ornament. He was in complete reaction against naturalistic or pictorial ornament, pointing out that the best ornament of the Japanese, Arabs and Indians was abstract. His designs are characterized by angular handles after the oriental, sometimes in ebony or wood, and functional shapes, in which decorative advantage was taken of joints and studs integral to the design. Typical is an arched toast rack in electro-plate, with six divisions on either side of a central vertical division, splayed out like a fan, the divisions made of electro-plated members, tubular in section and finished at their intersection with a plain ball head. He had a great feeling for the quality of his material as a covered claret jug of 1881 shows, in which gleaming deep bands of silver contrast with the different liquid gleam of the crystal glass. Many of Dresser's designs were carried out in electroplate as well as in silver; he trained assistants in his principles and firms for which he worked (Dixon's of Sheffield, Hulkin & Heath and Elkington's of Birmingham) brought out designs in his manner, so that silver in the Dresser style is worth looking for. Although an angularity which was elegance in Dresser's own designs, might become in other hands, a puritanical plainness, his work is a notable exception in a very dreary period. Dresser's work had an affinity with American design. For Tiffany's of New York he collected prototypes from Japan in 1867 and Tiffany's oriental designs in textured silver (not possible to produce in England as sterling) won a gold medal at the 1878 Paris Exposition. Chaffer's note on Tiffany's (History of Silver Makers) is interesting. In 1883 he observed a 'silver manufactory of five storeys, housing 400 workpeople, with a top floor designing room, large library and vast number of models! The designs he said were 'all original and no longer servile copies of the past, and had 'in fact, quite a style and flavour of the country'.

Late Victorian silver designs are best enjoyed and collected as forerunners of the modern movement. Their interest is often more historical than aesthetic, although select pieces by a designer such as Dresser have a quiet and subtle beauty of their own. These reservations apply less to the jewellery of the period than to any other department of design. Victorian jewellery from early until late can be a most satisfying thing to collect, and it can be collected at all levels, from the market junk stall to the West End auction rooms.

Some very horrid examples of Victorian taste in jewellery may be found, it is true, but on the whole the Victorian flair for detail and for producing charming small things is well displayed here. Victorian sentimentality reduced to so small a scale becomes a tender nostalgia. The most nostalgic period of all is the early period which Mrs Margaret Flower in her *Victorian Jewellery* calls the Romantic Period (1840-1860). With Mrs Flower's category of 'primary' jewellery, the truly state pieces using only precious stones, conceived in a grand style that was international in character, designed to be handed down as heirlooms, this book is only slightly concerned. The grand jewellers showing at the Great Exhibition such as Froment-Meurice from Paris, who designed fantastic Gothic bracelets in engraved gold and gold and enamelled pendants; John Brogden, who exhibited brooches decorated with motifs taken from the recent discoveries at Nineveh; A. W. Pugin, who also showed Gothic jewellery of the most charming design and many others, less original but highly professional, set the main characteristics of the style. The rest followed on, working in a wide range of less precious materials, but with effects equally charming.

The jewellery most worn in the period from 1840 to 1860 consisted mainly of brooches, rings and bracelets (in the forties, when hair covered the ears and a high neckline was fashionable, earrings and necklaces were less in fashion), followed in the next decade by diadems, necklaces and earrings with bracelets and brooches still in favour. The main stylistic divisions of the period round about 1851 were reproduced in miniature in the jewellery—there was a great deal of flowery rococo. Naturalism can be said to be represented by the snake bracelets, most realistically picked out in gold, with jewelled eyes, which curled round ladies' wrists (Queen Victoria had one, jewelled its whole twisted length), the flower and bird brooches, whilst there were also the gothic and archaeological styles. . . . A gothic tiara of fifteen little shapes like early English two-light windows, each with a pinnacle and trefoil on top, in gold and rubies with coloured enamels, was surprisingly light and pretty, whilst the rococo flowery tiaras produced by Watierston and Brogdon were quite as beautiful as any eighteenth-century work. Mildly archaeological interests were expressed in the brooches—gem cameos in the expensive ones, shell cameos in the cheaper. These shell cameos and the gems came originally from Italy, especially Rome, but by the time of the Great Exhibition they were being cut in London and Paris. The two large ones shown in Fig. 57 are in pink shell, the one in the gothic taste unmounted, probably English work and likely to date from the late forties. More rarely, other English cameos were made early in the period by Apsley Pellatt's 'sulphide' method of enclosing a white paste head in clear glass.

Comparable to the cameos are the lava medallions, with

Fig. 57. Two cameos in pink shell, one mounted as a brooch in gold. Both actual size, c. 1840 and probably English work.

classical heads white, beige, olive, grey, terracotta or chocolate in colour which were set as bracelets, brooches or rings in gold or silver. These, known as Pompeiian Jewellery, were brought back from Italian holidays. Some of the prettiest early Victorian holiday souvenirs, however, were the mosaic pieces brought back from Florence, Naples and Rome. The mosaic, made from minute chips of coloured stone, showed tiny views of Roman ruins, fiery horses' heads, lapdogs, birds on a branch and prettiest of all, flower bouquets. A very charming set, of black medallions with pink and white roses, bracelet, brooches and earrings, all set in gold, with vine leaves appliquéd, is illustrated in colour in Mrs Flower's *Victorian Jewellery*. Fig. 58 A shows a trinket box of comparable date, lined with oyster velvet, decorated with a spray of pinks in white and red against black. These mosaic pieces remained in favour for a long time, well into the mid-Victorian period. Fig. 59 shows a white violet against black, with leaves in two shades of green, and the plainness of its gold setting suggests the sixties or seventies. Coral jewellery was also brought back from Italy and coral was imported from Naples to London for fashioning by English jewellers. The pink and the red corals were most favoured and the coral was used for carved crosses, roses, hands, cameos and the like and made into bracelets, earrings and necklaces. A brooch made of a formal bouquet of coral rosebuds, accompanied by earrings of single rosebuds was particularly pretty. The Italians made their children necklaces of the branch corals to ward off the evil eye. English babies now wore branch coral or polished coral bead necklaces and cut their teeth on coral teething rings. Polished rings of coral were made into earrings.

Holidays nearer at hand provided souvenir jewellery. There was the Scottish vogue, made fashionable by the Queen and brooches of Cairngorm (smoky quartz with fine markings in red, brown or yellow) brought back from the Highlands were popular (Fig. 58, B), also Blue John from Derbyshire, malachite and moss agate. The stones were worked up into linked bracelets as well. Tiny fossils—such as coiled ammonites—were mounted as earrings. But the personal souvenir, the jewellery

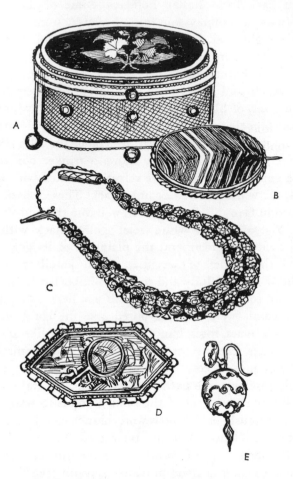

Fig. 58. A. Trinket box, gilt with mosaic top of a spray of pinks on a black ground: Italian c. 1840. B. Cairngorm brooch set in gold c. 1850. C. Pliable gold chain bracelet. c. 1850. C. Cut steel brooch with Japanese decoration c. 1888. E. Drop ear-ring in gold, with golden wire ornament, c. 1860.

The Norrington Flagon; silver with a London maker's mark: *c.* 1863. (*City Art Gallery, Plymouth*).

Silver tea and coffee service by Joshua Savery: London 1842. (*City Art Gallery, Plymouth*).

Paper weight in cut crystal: early or mid-Victorian. (*City Art Gallery, Plymouth*).

Two scent bottles: *Left*, painted glass with silver stopper: *c.* 1860. *Right*, porcelain with flowers in colour on a pink ground with enamelled gilt mountings: *c.* 1850. (*Buckland Abbey*).

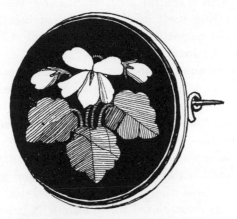

Fig. 59. Brooch. White violet against black background. Italian mosaic work, c. 1860.

of sentiment, was the most typical of the Romantic period. Brooches, even earrings and rings could be made to carry a message or remembrance of someone. The vogue for hair-work was at its height. Brooches were worked with romantic landscapes or flower pieces, set in a miniature gold frame like a tiny picture, entirely carried out in human hair. Hair was plaited and worked into twisted chains to form remarkably solid looking bracelets, generally with gold clasp and safety chain. Two shades of hair, woven together, probably intended a sentimental meaning. Brooches with gold rococo settings were fitted with equally rococo curls of hair, in one example light and dark hair has been curled into shapes like ostrich feathers; in another the woven strands of hair have been made into a somewhat bunchy bow, finished with gold tassels. Hair, often accompanied by seed pearls, was plaited and set in rings, which were made with a special hair-box in which the hair of one's own beloved might be placed.

The saddest little relics are the mourning rings, with the hair and pearls neatly picked out with a border of black

K

enamel, or with a central jewel of blackest Whitby jet, the band of the ring itself lined with plaited hair or simply a black and gold enamelled heart-shaped bezel, with a discreet little box at the back for the hair.

The delicacy and prettiness of the romantic period of Victorian jewellery is its highest merit. Workmanship was exquisite—the fidgetiness of hair-work must be seen to be imagined. Materials which led to delicate and detailed effects were in favour—rubies, sapphires, turquoise, amethyst, emeralds, diamonds, pearls and seed pearls amongst the gems. Seed pearls particularly were used in association with enamels and turquoise. Gold filigree was used a good deal and pliable gold chain was greatly used for bracelets. A bracelet such as the one in Fig. 58, C suggests the snake form so popular at the time in its rounded and pliable form. Despite the fineness of its detail, the jewellery was at all times characterized by a solid sturdiness of form. It was the best period: Mrs Flower's Grand Period (1860-1885) and the late Victorian or Aesthetic (1885-1901) have their merits, but nothing produced later has quite this artless charm.

Mrs Flower traces the difference in later Victorian jewellery that began to be apparent in the sixties as corresponding to a change in the position of women, who were now taking a much bolder and more definite part in life. In 1870 the Married Women's Property Act gave them control over the money which they earned themselves. Bolder and more flamboyant jewellery and more of it became the rule. In the fifties coronets and diadems had come in for wear at night and necklaces had become important once again. (Necklaces, except at night, were not much worn in the forties.)

By the sixties hair was being worn higher at the back and elaborate gold and jewelled combs came into fashion. Earrings had become long and dangling, sometimes with fringed droppers. Low necked dresses at the end of the decade brought lockets into fashion. Brooches and bracelets remained fashionable. A modest drop earring in plain gold, with golden wire ornament, is shown in Fig. 58, E.

Some really important jewellery was being made in the sixties and seventies by two very fine Italian jewellers, Castellani and Guiliano. They worked in the style of the high Renaissance which they understood perfectly. They matched their colours with dignity and restraint and produced pieces, particularly pendants with matching chains, which have a cold perfection. They used enamel work as a background to beautiful gems, often a cameo portrait (like the Marie de Medici by Guiliano in the Victoria and Albert Museum) or an intaglio (battle scene in sapphire in the Victoria and Albert, by Castellani). Even so, this work lacks the charm of the romantic period. The exuberance of the earlier fantasy has disappeared to be replaced by a slightly pedantic correctness. This was the state jewellery; the more ordinary jewellery was likewise less effective, although bolder in style.

This was the great age of gold, of large oval or circular brooches designed like shield bosses of gold, decorated with gold neatly beaded and surrounded with borders of cable twist with small jewels set in it. The gold was the important part, the jewels, often pearls or small diamonds looking small and a little poor in their setting. At its best the weighty boldness of the gold, a certain plainness, had a barbaric strength. This shows in the bracelets which are among the best things of their time: a broad and simple band of gold with three lotus flowers in appliqué, between sheaves of appliquéd gold wire, made somewhere about 1865 has a quiet excellence, whilst Richard Green's designs for the 1862 Exhibition have an almost chunky magnificence. Richard Green's brooches were as good as his bracelets: large bold cameos set in gold with classically moulded borders have an important look and so have circular or oval bracelets with a generously large central stone, surrounded by concentric rings of pearls. Another barbaric influence came from the East. There was

an Indian vogue, which expressed itself in parures made of
tiger's claws set in gold, necklace, earrings and all. Although
these are hardly in the taste of today, Indian bracelets such
as Fig. 60 have a certain outlandish elegance. The best of
the jewellery of the sixties was heavily magnificent, the worst
of it was slightly meagre in its plainness. The new techniques,
such as piqué, which was tortoiseshell with gold and silver
inlaid, could have a certain charm, but was often trivial and
stringy in its all over patterns. Stud earrings in piqué were
perhaps the prettiest way of using it. Whitby jet. which had
been originally used only for mourning, now gained a wider
vogue. Cameos and earrings were made in jet and heavy spiked
looking necklets, which resemble more barbaric versions of the
Bronze Age Irish gold necklaces. Polished balls of jet were
made up into necklaces and heavy jet neck chains with large

Fig. 60. Gold bracelet, c. 1860. Indian work.

links. Jet bracelets of coal black shiny snakes were worn. Light
and delicate things like seed pearls and hair were definitely
out, but rather horrid novelty jewellery of a light and stringy
meanness produced by machine at Birmingham, took its
place. In the eighties the gold that had a sort of sumptuous
plainness before was covered with feathery engraved patterns.
In simple lockets, this was pleasing enough but it was the
beginning of a new triviality in design. Fashionable influences
such as the Japanese were reflected in a summarily engraved
design, fitted on to an undeniably English shape, such as the
little brooch in Fig. 58, D.

For some time the Celtic element in design had been
apparent. It would be possible to collect Victorian jewellery
that shows its influence right through from the Great Exhibition onwards—late examples of ancient Irish jewellery
had inspired the exhibit of Messrs West of Dublin in 1851,
and the Scottish pebbles set in circles of silver in the eighteen-
sixties had further reflected the style, although heavier and
plainer. Now the Arts and Crafts movement, appalled by the
triviality of purely commercial jewellery, were to go back to
the Celtic for inspiration. But this was with an understanding of the principles of the style, not merely a borrowing of
motifs. C. R. Ashbee made some of the best of this Celtic
jewellery in his Essex House workshop, a great deal of it set
in silver. Ashbee's style in necklaces was to use large stones
such as moonstone in open silver settings, linked by a decorative chain in gold wire and enamels, using the celtic palmette
motif in the links. A silver chain set with moonstones uses
the palmettes paired, back to back to separate the stones.[1]
Ashbee's pendants and brooches were also light and uncluttered in design. One, an oval carbuncle surrounded by
amethysts and with a dropper of three amethysts, has the
jewels separated by round studs of silver, the whole finished
by a thin springing curved silver band, whilst another,

[1] Both these were made after a design by Hugh Seebohm. (c. 1896.)

extraordinarily modern in its asymmetrical plant decoration
which is almost abstract in feeling, has a design very close
to that of a Celtic minor-back. This is circular, made in silver,
with enamels and pearl blisters—a central pearl, a pearl above
the pendant set in palmettes and two pearls below, set either
side of a pearl dropper. Ashbee's designs reproduce the con-
tinuous moving linear curves of Celtic art most successfully.
Where the Celts used enamels and bronze, he used silver and
gemstones and enamel. The effect was never of a laboured antiquarian copy, but contemporary. For Ashbee's emphasis on
the gems themselves rather than the metal surrounding them
was characteristic also by now of the best commercial jewellery.

The eighties and nineties reacted against heavy gold settings and small gems by setting their jewels almost bare,
with light and finicky gold surrounds only. Traditional necklace shapes were challenged by the new dog-collar, made of
rows of vast numbers of small stones, pearls, or in cheaper
jewellery cut and polished jet. This was accompanied by a
long rope necklace. The long necklace perhaps showed a trace
of the aesthetic movement's influence, for Burne-Jones-type
ladies in the eighties had worn long strings of amber, garnet
or jet beads only, or perhaps a long and heavy silver chain
with a chased silver pendant of Japanese fish, or the ubiquitous dragon weaving itself in and out of the design. Hair was
worn high and jewelled, gold or silver pins were worn in it,
even by day. The vast cartwheel hats of the nineties were
also decked with pins, mostly embossed and engraved rather
meanly—though in garnet or enamels or jet outlined with
gold, or mother of pearl and gold they could be quite pretty.
Bracelets were worn by night and day, ostrich plumes set
in a jewelled aigrette in evening wear could take the place
of the vast day time hat. Diamonds were considered not the
thing by day, but at night, small diamonds worn scattered
in the hair or in a tiara, in a collar necklace and probably on

shoulder-knots, rings and bracelets as well, produced the maximum of sparkle. The emphasis of this fin-de-siècle commercial jewellery was on the display of gems, and settings are uninteresting. Rather horrid naturalistic butterflies and insects made their appearance, though delicious bits of nonsense like coiffure bows of spangled gauze bordered with tiny shells and wreaths of tinseled leaves and berries, were very pretty. Seed pearls became popular again and star brooches and pendants in seed pearls and small diamonds set in gold, vaguely neo-Georgian in design, are charming. Bracelets, which had still been of a satisfying breadth of gold at the end of the eighties became wire thin, mere settings for the ubiquitous diamonds and pearls. The century died out in a glitter of gems, pretty but rather ordinary.

The diamond-strewn grand jewellery of the last period of Victoria's reign will always be costly because of the intrinsic value of the gems. The cheaper hat-pins, rings, small brooches and clasps may be picked up in the junk shops. The art jewellery shading from Celtic to Art Nouveau is, however, worth collecting, a good deal of it beautiful in itself and important from the art history point of view. It could die away into atrocities of beaten silver and formalized flower-ornament, however, and some of Ashbee's more rugged pieces, especially his cloak and belt clasps, would be difficult to wear.

A fit ending to a plate and jewellery chapter is a few words on bric-à-brac, the small personal toys the Victorians liked collecting so much. The most important and valuable of these are the paper-weights. Even in their own day the French millefiori paper-weights from the St Louis, Clichy and Baccarat factories were highly prized; today they reach three-figure prices at the chief auction rooms. Even the Stourbridge imitations of Clichy are hardly likely to be cheap, or to be found in the junk stall tray. But they do occasionally turn up and are worth knowing about.

The millefiori process was originally Egyptian, then Roman

and carried from the ancient world to the modern by the Venetian glass makers, whose technique was copied by the French. It was a tortuous process, the tiny coloured canes like sticks of rock being each one very complicated to make, even more difficult when a figure—man, deer, dog, horse, butterfly or monkey—was required instead of a pattern. The individual canes, cut off in short lengths, sometimes a hundred at a time, were put cold into a mould with the required pattern, heated until the canes became welded together and withdrawn by a pontil rod to be coated with successive layers of crystal glass until the weight had been built up to size. Finally it had to be cooled very slowly in a kiln to remove all danger of cracking.

The Stourbridge copies of the French millefiori were based on those of the Paris factory at Clichy and it has been suggested that French workers from Clichy may have been imported to help in the manufacture, which started soon after the Vienna Exhibition of 1845. Stourbridge weights are different from the French in their proportions. They are larger, with a diameter of 3 to 4 inches and are semi-circular in section with a beaded rim at the base, whilst the French are elliptical. They are also simpler in their decoration—with five concentric rings of canes instead of seven, canes of the same colour in a ring and a central star. They copied Clichy designs, such as the turquoise or yellow basket set with coloured florets, or a central heart shaped ribbon of tartan twist, accompanied by a tartan twist border, but their colours were less bright than those of Clichy.

Anther type of paper-weight made in the mid-century by English glass makers was the flower weight, also an imitation of the French, but much cruder. Flowers in a pot made of coloured glass, generally in natural colour, were made by hand or moulded and covered by gatherings of crystal glass. Bubbles caused by air locks were used to simulate dewdrops on the leaves. Other paper-weights were formed of the Apsley Pellatt sulphides or 'crystallo-ceramics' as he called them—the white china clay paste busts of the famous looking like Wedgwood cameos enclosed in crystal glass. The Apsley Pellatt weights, made of the finest crystal, are very heavy and in their dignified plainness look just the thing for a gentleman's library table. Plain cut crystal weights like the one illustrated in Plate 41 occasionally turn up, or weights of polished quartz with interesting markings to please the collector of minerals.

Most of the bric-à-brac of the Victorian era, however, is essentially feminine in character. Three interesting fields for the collector, out of many, may be suggested—scent bottles, valentines and card cases. Scent bottles reflect all the fashions of their time, in china, glass and silver. Stourbridge made little millefiori scent bottles of a rather bulbous crystal glass shape with millefiori stopper and base: these were in imitation of Clichy. The circular willow pattern bottle with silver mounting in Plate 42 probably also dates from the forties. On the same photograph the tiny bottles to slip in a purse or reticule are also early, but the larger cut glass bottle with silver top probably dated from the cut glass revival of the eighties or nineties. The china bottle with enamelled gilt top and butterfly stopper (Plate 32) is probably Great Exhibition period. Its flower painting is delightful, in natural colours, but the anchovy pink ground above the main panel of decoration is a little excessive. Beside it stands a discreetly painted Gothic glass bottle, a little later in date, perhaps of the sixties. Scent bottles come in all shapes and sizes and make an amusingly varied collecion.

Valentines are often frankly absurd. The early ones maybe robustly humorous à la Cruikshank and *Punch* or sweetly pretty, with coloured moss roses, lily of the valley and forget-me-not surrounded by paper lace and bathetic verse. They are often ingeniously folded, to conceal secret inscriptions. Later ones are just as artless, but much more fussy. At Buckland Abbey there is a heavily tinselled specimen of the eighties

or nineties, with a tiny message 'From a True Love' attached
to a little bouquet of artificial lilies of the valley and what look
like china rose buds, so embowered with paper lace, tinsel and
ribbon as to be hardly visible. Even in the sophistication of
the nineties, the valentine was just as silly and simple, if more
novel in its presentation. In the same collection there is one
made into a little fan, with swansdown and plated handle.
Concealed inside, behind the angelic child (who is very nicely
drawn in a Kate Greenaway manner), is the secret loving
message.

Of Victorian trinkets there is no end. Card cases are charming things to collect, beautifully made in mother of pearl,
inlaid ivory and ebony or tortoise shell. The examples most
often found probably date from the sixties and seventies.
Examples of tortoise-shell decorated with scatters of mother of
pearl flowers in the Japanese taste are probably later. The
influence of oriental and native work during the period would
be an interesting theme to follow a great deal of Indian
jewellery came into the country and sailors brought back
beautiful examples of native craftsmanship from their
journeys—like the unassuming looking stripy workbox of
Fig. 61, which is actually very nicely made of porcupine quills,

Fig. 61. Work box. Of porcupine quills and ebony inlaid,
native work.

with every kind of fitting and drawer inside, laboriously and beautifully finished. Smaller and less elaborate porcupine quills boxes sometimes turn up.

Nothing more unlike the laborious native craftsmanship could be imagined than the ingenious and sometimes slightly absurd efforts of English amateurs. But the Victorian age with its rising standard of living and increased leisure for the large families of the middle classes, was the age *par excellence* of the amateur. Wood carving was probably the most popular craft and its elaborations by the professional

Fig. 62. Shell and cork work picture, c. 1860. The picture made of starfish, crab, sea urchin, coralline weeds, etc., the frame of cork with insets of deep red velvet and shell basket and limpet decoration, gilt rebate.

were to be seen on many stands at the Great Exhibition, decorating furniture with enormous still lifes, or shown on its own as a *tour de force* of naturalism.

Amateur work is luckily less elaborate and some pleasant-textured and relatively simple designs may be found, such as dishes, bread boards and so on. Allied to wood carving, but at the same time sharing the picture-making qualities of Berlin wool-work, was shell or cork work. Fig. 62 shows an elaborate example dating back to the fifties or early sixties. The frame is of cork, with red velvet insets, decorated at each of the four corners with a limpet shell. The shell picture is built up of real shells and dried sea weeds. Although over-elaborate, the textures and colours are charming. This, and allied crafts such as modelling flowers in bread and wax, although they sound unpromising, sometimes bring forth very decorative 'primitive' effects, surprisingly rich in texture.

CHAPTER IX

ENVOI: VICTORIANA IN THE GARDEN

THE VICTORIANS as gardeners have been much maligned. Carpet bedding immediately springs to mind with laurels and monkey puzzle trees in the background. Actually Victoria's reign was the period when the great collectors brought trees and shrubs from India, South America, New Zealand, Tasmania and later China, now taken for granted in our gardens. It was also the period for florist's flowers—auriculas, pinks, tulips and fuchsias—for formal flowered shrubs, such as *camellia japonica* and for roses of an elegance never surpassed. There were styles of garden layout other than carpet bedding pure and simple; Loudon's pleasing romanticism, like the setting of a Taglioni ballet early in the period; and, in reaction to the formal bedding school, later in the century William Robinson and Gertrude Jekyll, with their wild woodland gardens and impressionist colour schemes. From the forties onwards the great Cornish gardens were developing —glades of rhododendrons, magnolia, camellia were growing up to make the exotic jungles of their maturity. Glendurgan, Trelissick, Rosehill, Caerhays, Ludgvan, Tregrehan, Menabilly and Carclew were great romantic gardens, quite beyond carpet bedding in their scope.

The great Victorian gardens are also quite beyond our scope in their maintenance. Their scale, even in the woodland gardens, demanded a large skilled staff and constant care. But we can re-discover the elegance and quality of the plants they grew by collecting them and enjoy, by judicious selec-

tion, the romantic fantasy of their garden furniture and ornaments.

Victorian garden furniture and, to a less degree, garden
figures, have become rare and much sought after. Many of
the figures probably disappeared in the intense reaction
against anything Victorian suffered by the generations immediately following. The garden furniture, mostly cast iron,
has undergone the purges of two wars and their demand for
metal. What remains is now very fashionable and commands
high prices.

Both figures and furniture, however, may still be found
occasionally at country house sales. Tremendous set pieces
of garden statuary, like the Perseus fountain at Witley Court,
Worcestershire, and the prehistoric beasts which are the
wonders of the Crystal Palace, are, of course, completely useless in a modern setting.

But single figures and especially small garden beasts have
a Tenniel-esque charm. Most often seen are the terracotta
eagles with spread wings. The bird illustrated (Fig. 63) came
from a Cornish garden planted in the eighteen-sixties. No
great work of art as a figure, he is at the same time a comfortable guardian presence of a size just right to place under a
cedar tree, or to close a small vista or even to dominate a
small town garden. The sentimental pseudo-classical parian
or the full scale marble of Royal Academy pieces look so
much better translated into coade stone or terracotta, having
collected a decent patina of weathering and some romantic
moss and lichen. Typical is the sentimental girl and dog
from the same Cornish garden, probably designed c. 1850-60
and very much in the style of the parian figures made for
indoors (Fig. 64, C). Some pleasing, if rather heavy, vases
were made throughout the period. In weighty rows deployed
along terraces, overlooking laboriously wrought knot gardens
or planted with bedding-out exotics they looked solid and
overwhelming. Used one at a time in a small garden the

Fig. 63. Eagle. In terracotta on larva base, c. 1860.

simpler examples can be very pleasing (Fig. 64, A, B).

Victorian garden furniture of the earliest phase was, following indoor fashion, fattened Georgian in style. A watercolour of the Whiteford children in the eighteen-fifties playing in their grandfather's Plymouth garden shows the usual stucco villa, a lawn, a charming glass house and a white-painted garden seat with a lattice back reminiscent of a simplified

Fig. 64. A, B, Garden urns. Late Victorian. A. Terracotta, B. Coade stone. C. Garden figure group: *Girl and Dog*. c. 1850. In coade stone.

eighteenth-century Chinese Chippendale. Jane and Claudius Loudon, whose *Encyclopaedia of Farm and Village Cottage Architecture* came out first in 1833, but was repeatedly re-issued during the forties and fifties, showed designs for garden furniture which were heavier than the Georgian but still preserved a memory of its good proportion. The bark-encrusted rustication of some of it is too likely to provide a home for earwigs but it has, nevertheless, a slightly comic charm. This taste for a heavy rustic style persisted right through the period, the rustic bench in its romantic naturalism appealing to William Robinson in the nineties as much as it did to the villa gardeners of the forties and fifties.

Those dark nostalgic pavilions, the summer houses and summer-seats where Victorian ladies took tea in the shade, or sat on quiet evenings, were furnished either with rustic wood, or from the forties onwards with cast iron garden seats and later, cast iron tables and chairs. The rococo detail of current fashions in mahogany translated into cast iron produced garden seats of a charm the weighty mahogany never possessed. Their elaboration gives them the engaging qualities of a folly. Their absurd design and cluttered motifs take on an iced cake prettiness with a coat of white paint. The cast iron has a pleasing quality of texture, even under paint. Hence they are popular as modern garden features and although they were produced in their hundreds, correspondingly rare.

From about 1840, the large iron foundries in Ireland, Scotland, Coalbrookdale and Birmingham poured out garden seats and occasional furniture. One of the prettiest garden seats came from the Waterford factory; a traditional frenchified sofa shape, the back carried out in a filigree of fernleaves. If purists like Sir Charles Eastlake would have disapproved of its rococo curves, the hectic proliferation of acanthus swags and restive curved mouldings on legs, arms and cresting of the Carron Company of Stirlingshire's design of 1846, would have pleased him even less. This particular seat[1] had a back of linked mouldings producing a chainmail or fish scale effect. This linked moulding has just a suggestion of a much later development in garden furniture, when in the eighties and nineties it was made in tube, strap-metal or wire, echoing more attractively the shapes of current drawing-room designs. Miss Aslin illustrates two very charming wire chairs, of French bergère shape with catherine wheel twists forming

---

[1] It is illustrated by Elizabeth Aslin, *Nineteenth Century English Furniture*, plate 48.

L

seat and back made by Barnard, Bishop and Barnard of Norwich (c. 1880). The ingenuity of these workmanlike designs shows the Victorians at their best, for they are nearer engineering functionalism than anything else. Tubular metal was made into garden hammocks, gaily striped and with swinging fringes and tassels, an elaborate system of jointed metal rods supporting the whole. Hardly less functional in their way were the bast and bamboo curlicued chaise longues of the eighties, well adapted for Tissot-like ladies in bustles and muslins to recline upon in summer on the terrace, in winter in conservatories and winter gardens.

The later pieces of garden furniture are less likely to be sought after than the early. The simple solid style fashioned by William Robinson and Gertrude Jekyll at the very end of the period, plentifully illustrated in the *English Flower Garden*, produced pleasing unobtrusive furniture, most of it in oak or stone. But if simple, it tends to be rather massive in character for the modern small garden. A white painted 7-legged wooden seat with semi-circular slatted back—of which there is a cut in the *English Flower Garden*—is typical. It is an agreeable piece, if a trifle long legged and high in the back, but definitely designed for a large number of people in a large space. Nevertheless, this furniture is worth searching for at country house sales. The decadent cottagey rustic style which followed aped its cottage airs without its integrity.

If Victorian garden furniture tends to be rare and difficult to come by, Victorian plants provide a much easier quarry. They are amongst the most satisfying of Victoriana to collect, for the Victorians were great plantsmen. The flowers they bred perfectly expressed the characteristic taste of each period of the reign, but always in its most endearing manifestations. Many of them may still be found in specialist nurserymen's lists, others wait to be re-discovered in old gardens. The habit of inspecting the site of a derelict cottage, of acquiring a lynx-eye for garden material when old houses are being demolished in a town is as worth getting as is an eye for the contents of junk-shops. Many a plant rescued by means of cuttings or suckers from a ruined cottage garden has proved of very rewarding beauty—and sometimes of more vigour than its stock.

All periods of the Victorian age were rich in exotic flowers, as the great plant collectors brought back their treasures from abroad to be grown in the gentle climates of the West and South West: Sir Joseph Hooker with his Indian and Himalayan rhododendrons in the forties, William Lobb and his associates with South American plants, and others from the Antipodes and South Africa, or to be tried under glass like the monster 'Victoria Regia' waterlily flowered for the first time by Paxton at Chatsworth. The plant breeders at home too produced their own wonders, reproducing almost exactly the bouquets of the porcelain painters in the flowers of the garden. The early and middle periods produced the florist's flowers, the two later decades, following William Robinson's reaction against formality the best of the specifically garden varieties which survive today. The artisan florists, searching for symmetry of form and marking were as good gardeners in their way as William Robinson and his friends, who were looking for a natural, wilder grace and in doing so, reviled the strict formal shapes and fantastic streaked and spotted flowers of the florists.

Of the old florist's flowers the easiest to obtain are the tulip, fuchsia and pelargonium, zonal and regal. The rose, although hardly a florist's flower, shared some of their formality in the earlier periods, as did the camellia and azalea. Tulips and fuchsias are the easiest to collect. One specialist firm keeps a separate hand-list of the old English florist's tulips and at least one other firm of tulip specialists carries a few varieties. If not listed on their own as Old English Tulips they may be found amongst the bizarres and bybloemens catalogued with the late flowering varieties.

The old English show tulip has a refinement lost by the coarser Darwin. Whilst the Darwin is flat based and square in silhouette, the old English varieties are goblet shaped, with symmetrically overlapping petals to form as perfectly round a rim as possible. They may be flamed or feathered, or plain coloured breeders (i.e. the varieties from which the flamed and feathered ones broke). Flaming should spread out from the base in wide flakes of colour as evenly as possible. Feathering is marking from the edge of the petals inward. Bizarres are flamed and feathered with a colour dark on a lighter ground, bybloemens light on a dark ground. A variety that is easy to get and a good doer is 'Sam Barlow'. A bizarre, flamed an almost black-brown on a strong straw yellow, is a tiger of a flower, marked with great refinement and distinctness. Raised in 1856, it looks back to the eighteenth century in its restraint for it is not gaudy. It reminds me in form of the striped tulips illustrated in Thornton's *Temple of Flora*, in the seventeen-nineties. 'Sir Joseph Paxton' is another good one, a lighter, tawnier brown against its yellow background. 'Black Boy', a bybloemen feathered yellow on two shades of brown and black, has a sulky beauty. It lasts long in the garden without going off and is a magnificent foil for other colours (notably the chalky-purply modern Darwins). 'Columbine', pink on white, introduced in the sixties and 'May Blossom', neatly feathered red on white, have a laundered prettiness that is fresh and attractive. In contrast to these early Victorian flowers there are one or two garden varieties amongst the may-flowering and lily-flowered tulips, recommended by Robinson and well worth having today. 'Picotee', a white lily-flowering tulip, has a neat pink edge which deepens and spreads as the flower ages. 'Gala Beauty' (syn. *Columbus*) yellow, edged red and 'Retroflexa', scarlet, may still be found in ordinary trade lists. 'Gala Beauty' is a small tulip, very late in the season but of particularly beautiful form and bright yet soft colouring. It is not gaudy, as its name might suggest and it lasts in beauty, both cut and in the garden for a long time. They are the first of a great class of lily-flowered tulips, like the incomparable yellow lily-flowered 'Mrs Moon' (before 1900—named after the wife of a botanical painter) which are proven garden plants of hard constitution; indeed 'Mrs Moon' is a gentle spreader, invading ground by means of stolons.

The florist's tulips should be treated with care and respect like all show flowers. 'Black Boy' is persistent enough, but after two or three years the others will probably deteriorate and stocks have to be renewed. Not so the fuchsia, for the Victorian varieties, with a few exceptions, are the most vigorous of all Victorian plants. A great number, literally a hundred or so, of varieties survive. Amongst these, the smaller varieties of delicate shape and refinement of colour date from the early period, novel colours of rather garish hue characterize the mid-Victorian introductions, whilst the sumptuous giant show flowers, reminiscent of the conservatories of the eighties and nineties were introduced late in the reign. Many of these late ones have a foreign looking elegance and were indeed raised abroad by nurserymen such as Rozain-Bourcharlet, Lemoine and Cornelissen.

Originally thought of as indoor or conservatory plants, or as half hardy bedders, the fuchsia has shown itself far hardier than the Victorians supposed. Many of them may stay outdoors all the years round, particularly the early Victorian varieties, which are compact and bushy in habit and which, although they may be cut to ground level in a hard winter, will generally spring again, giving finer if later flowers on the young wood. They will be quite safe and will root below frost level if given a lavish dressing of spent hops and peat well down, which they love and root into. A top dressing of cinders, or bracken and leaves, drawn well up amongst the bottom growth gives protection and a start to the young shoots.

In the South Western coastal districts *fuchsia magellanica* and *Riccartonii* make tree-like shrubs and are used for hedging; even the delicate, late Victorian large-bloomed fuchsias will survive. Further away from the sea over-winter protection is advisable. In general the early Victorians are probably best for ordinary border purposes but some of the later varieties are hardy enough. I give a small selection from all periods, all more or less hardy. 'Chillerton Beauty' (syn. 'General Tom Thumb'—but not to be confused with 'Tom Thumb', which was a later introduction) should come first, since it was a favourite of Queen Victoria's and grown at Osborne. Raised by Bassin in 1847, its tube and sepals are pale rose pink, its corolla or 'skirt' of petals mauvish violet; it is slightly larger than 'Tom Thumb' (1850) which is also a good, hardy and floriferous plant with carmine sepals and mauve corolla, sufficiently dwarf in character for use on the larger slopes of a rock garden, with a compact and discreet charm which is delightful anywhere. Another small and hardy plant, with a strong period flavour is 'Venus Victrix' (1840) tube and sepals white-tipped green, corolla violet. It is not as free as some, but as the first variety raised with white sepals, it has an historical interest. I have grown neither 'Venus Victrix' or 'Dunrobbin Bedder' (1890), but both are rated hardy and 'Dunrobbin Bedder', bright scarlet and dark purple and described as 'spreading, dwarf and hardy', was raised in one of the great house gardens as an efficient edging plant in bedding schemes. Taller and more elegant, in fact with a sumptuous enough flower to make one doubt her hardiness, is the redoubtable 'Mrs Popple' (1899). With scarlet tube and sepals and dark violet corolla, this is an excellent all purpose garden fuchsia and seems as hardy as the hedging fuchsias here in the South West. An earlier type, in habit perhaps more decorative from a garden point of view, is 'Madame Cornelissen', tall and branchy with pointed elegant leaves and soft scarlet pagodas with turned back pointed sepals and white skirts. This most amiable of plants will flower right into winter. 'Ballet Girl', raised by Veitch in 1894, is typical of its period in its elegance. Difficult to get true to name and doubtfully hardy, it is a first class show flower with rich cerise tube and sepals and white corolla, veined with cerise. 'Amy Lye' (1885) is in colour slightly sickly and only too true to a certain failure of taste in its period, its tube and sepals waxy white, its 'skirt' coral-orange. It is counted half hardy to hardy. 'Caledonia' (1899) has upright, slender and graceful growth and is hardy enough. Its colour is pleasing, with tube and sepals cerise, corolla reddish violet. 'Pumila', a most charming miniature, with frail-looking upright branches, sharp sealing wax red and purple tiny flowers, is a miniature column of flower. It has survived some toughish winters with me, but may be less hardy up country.

To the Victorians, the rose was the queen of flowers. Each period of the reign has its characteristic blooms, the formal and elegant full petalled flowers of the earlier years giving way to the luscious, if rather heavy, hybrid perpetuals of the middle and late periods of the reign; with the slightly frail and more elegant, high centred tea roses of the fifties and sixties generally being replaced by their more bouncing and less fastidious relations, the hybrid teas, in the nineties. The hybrid sweet briers, the rugosas and other shrub roses in their informal freedom were as typical of the Robinsonian naturalism in gardening which invaded the last years of the century as the delicate formality of the Bourbon so-called 'Shell Rose' 'Madame Pierre Oger' is the apotheosis of the elegance of the earlier decades. While many of the less vigorous kinds have been lost to cultivation, many survive and a large selection from all periods may be found in specialist nursery lists. Those which have survived, unnoticed and still to be re-discovered, in old gardens, are certainly vigorous enough to come from Irishman's cuttings or suckers, or with care, from ordinary July cuttings.

Best propagated from suckers or Irishman's cuttings are the oldest types of Victorian roses, non-perpetual, flowering in one glorious flush of bloom early in June and then not at all for the rest of the season. These are mostly Victorian seed-lings of the established varieties of the old garden rose—Damasks, Gallicas, Centifolias and, most typical of the early Victorians, the nostalgic Moss. Most of them, not all, are hardy enough to survive conditions which modern bedding roses would certainly not abide. Their subtle, gentle colours and formal, camellia like shape, above all their really delicious scent, make them amongst the most desirable of Victorian roses.

Like the furniture and china of the forties these roses are really improvements on the eighteenth century types. 'Madame Legras de St Germain', for instance, a quartered white Damask rose with a faint cream flush at heart—was an attempt at producing a yellow rose without recourse to Persian yellow or tea rose blood. About the same date is the deep purple Gallica 'Cardinal Richelieu' (1840) a refinement on all the purple roses. This is a most shapely rose with per-fectly finished flowers, frilled with petals, quartered, often with a green eye, of subtle dusky colour, fading almost to parma violet as it ages. Perhaps best of the Victorian Gallicas, this lasts longest in water and is decorative at all stages, from its knobby round reddish bud to its final grey-purple demise. 'Cardinal Richelieu' has very dark rounded leaves and an open habit of growth. 'Charles de Mills' has much the same elegance of shape, goblets of wine-red with deepest dusky crim-son in the centre petals. These Gallicas with their formal flowers and neat leaves, form a shapely whole. Lacking the blowsy vigour of the Hybrid Perpetuals or the slightly over-hanging heads of the delicate Teas, they have a balanced per-fection of stem, leaf and flower which the more sumptuous later beauties cannot match.

The Moss Roses share this exquisite balance and have the

added beauty of their richly mossed buds. The Moss is the most typical Victorian of all the old 'summer roses'[1] adding to the eighteenth-century felicity of shape and colour, varieties with a certain sentimental elegance and even a mild eccentricity of manners very much of its period. Even their names have a slightly dotty elegance (usually French); 'Nuits de Young' (1851) is an example. Perhaps named for Young's *Night Thoughts*—a popular bedside book—this is a little bush of deepest velvety purple, with little dark leaves. It was a great favourite of Mrs Constance Spry, as were the much more vigorous clear pinks, 'Jeanne de Montfort' and the sumptuous 'General Kleber'. The paragon or mosses to me, is however, 'Wiliam Lobb'—tall, vigorous, of a delicate parma violet colour and with handsome velvety flowers—almost as elegant as those of 'Cardinal Richelieu'. This is a princely rose and well named in honour of the great Victorian gardener and plant hunter.

Apart from these aristocrats there are many forgotten Moss Roses to be found in old gardens, sometimes rather a mallow or purple pink, a little cabbagey, but all sweet scented, long suffering of neglect and with an indefinable period charm.

The basic stud roses of the nineteenth century, however, from which all the typical Victorian developments of rose-breeding sprang, are the China or so-called Monthly roses. These brought about a great improvement: they were per petual flowering. The 'Autumn' Damasks had produced a few flowers after the first great flush of June was over, but these truly flowered from early summer until the frosts. From the China roses crossed with others came the Bourbons, the Hybrid Perpetuals and the Hybrid Teas—the Victorian foundation of the modern bedding roses. Chinese garden roses were first imported in the seventeen-nineties, and the earliest developments from them were the Bourbons, Chinas, Bour-

---

[1] Although the basic types of Moss rose were actually introduced in the eighteenth century.

bon Noisettes (also with China blood) and Tea roses, the aristocrats of mid-Victorian times, gradually superseded by the more sumptuous and vigorous Hybrid Perpetuals and Hybrid Teas more typical of the late Victorian taste. Seedlings of the original Chinas were, however, bred right through to late Victorian times—they never lost favour as garden roses, though the florists might deplore their loose silky flowers and variable colour; both William Paul in 1898, and the great William Robinson commended them as garden plants.

As William Robinson found, the Chinas are invaluable as garden shrubs. They are probably the easiest of the old roses to fit in with a modern garden scheme, because of their very informality. They are much more suitable to be planted with shrubs than the very domesticated and formal summer roses. Also their leaves and young growth are extremely decorative —often bronzed and always shapely in habit. 'Fellemburg', with crimson-pink rounded flowers in clusters and a slender growth of bronzed foliage on long shoots (it can be trained to a wall) is typical of the early seedlings. At their best 'Fellemburg's' flowers have a decidely Chinese look—like the neat little roses on the oriental cups and saucers brought back by Victorian sea captains. 'Blairii No. 2' (the first of Mr Blair's seedlings has not survived) is even more vigorous, with really coppery young growth and delightful clear pink flowers. A later China, typical of the more sumptuous taste of the sixties is 'Rival de Paestum', raised by G. Paul in 1863. It has foliage and young shoots which Mr Graham Thomas[1] describes as 'rich glorious plum' and 'long creamy buds' which 'nod to open into loose, semi-double ivory white blooms'; the 'Rival' has a slight tea scent. 'Laurette de Messimy' (illustrated in William Robinson's *The English Flower Garden*) is typical of late Victorian taste. A French rose bred in 1887 with the

[1] Graham Stuart Thomas: *The Old Garden Roses.*

Fig. 65. Roses—early and mid-Victorian. A. 'Madame Pierre Oger';
B. Moss, 'Capt. John Ingram' (note bud); C. 'Reine des Violettes';
D. China—'Fellemberg'; E. 'Commandant Baurepaire'; and F. White
Scots Briar.

'Rival' as one parent, it is salmon-pink, shaded copper and
yellow and with a yellow base. The later Victorians were fas-
cinated by these breaks towards flame and salmon-pinks, the
novelty of vivid, rather un-rose like colours. On the other hand
'Gruss-an-Teplitz' brought out by Lambert of Trier in 1897,
is that most rose like of colours, a deep dark crimson, with a

spicy scent and strong arching shoots with purplish foliage becoming green later on. This rose was another of Constance
Spry's favourites, which speaks for its quality. The flowers
borne in clusters, are of a velvety darkness and richness and
its sumptuous colour and scent make it typical of its time,
with a rather *fin de siècle* elegance.

Mr Graham Thomas would regard 'Gruss-an-Teplitz' as a
Bourbon despite its great proportion of Chinese blood, too
crossbred to count as China. The Bourbons, however, produced some of the loveliest roses of the Victorian era,
characteristic of the early period with their formally beautiful flowers, relying on delicacy of colour and shape for their
charm rather than on the full blooded lavishness of some
of the later beauties. They arose from a cross between an
Autumn Damask (i.e. the old pink Damask which produced
a few flowers in the autumn as well as in June) and 'Parson's
Pink China' and were developed from a chance seedling found
on the Île de Bourbon in 1817. One of the prettiest and most
typical is 'Louise Odier' (1851). A clear pink with a very
rounded, full petalled flower, this is a rose which looks just
like the pink roses which appear on so much of the porcelain
(c. 1840-1850). Delicious cut—it is very sweet—it looks pleasant growing, with slender twiggy growth and very clean,
pointed light green foliage which shows its China ancestry.
Not a large rose, it is floriferous and easy, looking after itself
in far from favourable circumstances in my Cornish garden.
Much more aristocratic and a little delicate as well is 'Madame
Pierre Oger', the shell-rose, and 'La Reine Victoria', the pink
rose from which she sported, is hardly less so. With perfectly
shaped cupped blooms, filled with petals, these are the most
perfect of Victorian roses. They come late in their period,
'La Reine' in 1872 and 'Madame Pierre' in 1878 and perhaps
they are almost too perfect, a little frail, with almost trans-
parent petals, and delicate scent, but although their growth
is upright and slender, they are much stronger than they

look. 'Madam Pierre' is an early rose, in a warm spring opening with the late tulips her blush-white blooms flushed with pink, held upright on slender stems, with very pretty light green leaves, saw-toothed red. Although a good deal tougher than she looks, in a good season she can be a martyr to black spot and needs spraying early. Despite black spot, however, which comes well after the first flush of bloom, 'Madame Pierre' is truly perpetual, carrying a few flowers until the frosts spoil them. Other Bourbons worth growing are 'Tour de Malakoff'—a soft parma violet shaded rose—and 'Madame Lauriol de Barny'—a lavish flowering silvery pink—both advocated by Mrs Spry. Her stripy favourites—'Tricolour de Flandres', 'Variegata di Bologna' and 'Honorine de Brabant', with their streaks and splashes of crimson and purple on white, may not be to everyone's liking, but are very typical of a certain freakishness in Victorian taste. 'Commandant Beaurepaire' is another striped rose, of charming soft colour, but unfortunately never happy in my Cornish garden.

Comparable to 'Madame Pierre' in elegance is 'Reine des Violettes' (1860), a soft violet-purple rose of cupped and rounded shape, full petalled, formal, and yet graceful and charming. This makes a large bush, with smooth leaden-green leaves, and is a truly perpetual flowerer. The buds open grape-purple at first, and the flower lightens as it ages to parma violet, always with a difference in colour between the upper surfaces and the light silky reverses of the petals. It needs good soil, in which it will grow up to six feet. 'Reine des Violettes', however, is classed not as a Bourbon, but as a Hybrid Perpetual—an early seedling of the race, which, with the Hybrid Teas, drove the old roses out of the garden.

'Madame Isaac Perrière' (1880), however, classed as a Bourbon, has the weight and slight crudeness of colour, the buxom vigour generally associated with the Hybrid Perpetuals. This is a typical late Victorian rose, madder red, with a suggestion of plush about colour and texture, stout stems and a slightly

larger leaf than the older Bourbons. Lavish in bloom, prac-
tically unkillable, with enormous, sweetly scented flowers,
this is a most generous rose. The flower, slightly cabbagey,
lacks the shapeliness of the earlier types. 'Madame Isaac' has
more kinship in appearance with the large and rich, slightly
vulgar, hybrid perpetuals which were being introduced by
this time in their hundreds, than with the more delicate and
restrained Bourbons. But what exuberance the hybrid perpetuals, the late Victorian's own particular roses have! Great
cane like shoots, often better pegged down to soil surface to
make them break into hoops of bloom, with large rounded
vigorous light green leaves and high centred cabbagey flowers,
lavish in scent and colour, are characteristic of 'Mrs John
Laing' (blandly pink, 1887) 'Fisher Holmes' (1856, scarlet
lake and very vigorous) 'Ulrich Brunner fils' (1882, cerise
shaded lilac) and 'General Jasqueminot' (1853, a large cabbagey and very sweet crimson). 'General Jasqueminot',
although early in date, was more characteristic of the new
style in roses than the old, and Dean Hole (who had the
honour of a very fine dark red H.P. rose named after him
(1860), regarded the 'General' in high honour as one of the
best red garden roses many years after .

The frontispiece to Dean Hole's *Book about Roses* (1870) is
a nicely coloured lithograph of his name rose, 'Reynolds
Hole'. This high centred, heavy rose is rich in colour, a dark,
shaded crimson and large in size. It completely lacks the
refinement of shape of the early Victorian 'summer' roses.
Neither were the later hybrid perpetuals graceful in growth.
Their excessive vigour produced gawky, heavily thorned
bushes. Pictures by Spencer Gore and Bevan show their legacy
to the Edwardians—a dazzle of summer heat in a garden and
a background of knobbly bushes growing these great sumptuous silky flowers at the end of long whippy stems. 'Frau
Karl Druschki' (1901) with its awkward growth is an example
—but the pure cold whiteness of the high centred flowers make

it extremely valuable. 'Frau Karl', introduced in the last year of our period, is still easily obtainable from nurserymen; Mr Graham Thomas reckons it still the most beautiful white rose ever raised, although it lacks scent.

'Frau Karl' was bred from a famous pink tea rose, 'Caroline Testout'—again still to be found in some catalogues, though most often in the climbing form. 'Caroline Testout', raised in the eighties, traced back to the large silvery pink 'La Reine' (1842). This has disappeared, but 'La France' (1867) a most refined and beautiful silvery pink, still appears in specialist catalogues. 'La France' was half tea, half hybrid perpetual and one of the forerunners of the modern hybrid teas, more elegant in growth than the H.P.'s and stronger than the tea roses. For the tea roses, like other mid-Victorian beauties, were liable to go into a decline. Protected by conservatories and winter gardens, fed on elaborate mixtures of compost and rich manure, they demanded constant care to be kept in good health. They were typical of the lavish upper-class living of the sixties and seventies when cohorts of gardeners served elaborate green houses and time could be given to a strict routine of cultivation and training. Dean Hole gives receipts for their care in his book. Such beauties as the climbers 'Marechal Neil, Devoniensis' (a fine yellow raised by Vietch in the forties), and 'Niphetos' were only for the fortunate few. 'Niphetos', a cold white with greenish shading, is the epitome of its period; in leaf, stem and flower, this has an incomparable elegance, opening from a beautiful long pointed bud. But it is a frail rose, it hangs its head and the fresh green stems are brittle and slender. In the West, 'Devoniensis' is probably hardy enough on a wall, but 'Niphetos' really needs the protection of glass to keep the delicate white petals unspotted. 'Gloire de Dijon', pinkish buff with an orangey heart, is a stouter member of the family, but has finally succumbed in my Cornish garden—probably of old age, as it was planted nearly a century ago.

In the last decade of the century, what might be called the naturalistic style of gardening, advocated by William Robinson, came into its own, in reaction to the formality of carpet bedding with annuals, tender shrubs and exotics which had prevailed in the past. Although the climate of appreciation was slow to change, the emphasis was now on plants as material to clothe a garden landscape. Various roses, climbers, ramblers and first crosses from species began to come into their own. Some had been cherished for years in cottage gardens and in such gardens as Charles Kingsley's Rectory at Eversley, and now found champions in William Robinson and Gertrude Jekyll; others were new introductions from plant hunting expeditions in South America, India, China or the Antipodes, or were specially bred for their garden qualities. The 'Penzance Briars' were bred specially for the new informal gardening. They were hybrid briars with a cross of Persian yellow blood, most noticeable in the colour of the pair 'Lord and Lady Penzance', named for their originators. Others had names from Scott— such as 'Jeannie Deans' (crimson scarlet, semi-double with aromatic foliage), and 'Amy Robsart' (deep rose pink, semi-double). One of the most beautiful hybrid briars seems to have originated as a chance seedling in a hedgerow, however, 'Janet's Pride', with romantic semi-double flushed cherry-pink and white flowers, each with a central golden boss of stamens and grey green glaucous briar foliage, faintly aromatic. Informal shrubby roses, like the Rugosa crosses so popular in the nineties and vigorous climbers—ramblers which could scramble up the pillars and across the rafters of Robinsonian pergolas—were raised. These rugosas, which make large thrifty mounds of crinkled light green foliage, have gloriously scented flowers and are more or less perpetual flowering, many of them, the singles at least, carrying large tomato-like hips at the same time as their autumn crop of flowers. They are especially useful for gardens where conditions are not suitable for the more tender kinds of rose. They will grow in the tougher climate of the New World and they will tolerate semi shade, and bear conditions few of the more highly bred garden roses would stand. And their flowers, if informal, do not lack quality. 'Blanc double de Coubert' raised in 1892 by Cochet-Cochet is typical, with slender buds as neat and slim as a furled umbrella, slightly blush tinted, opening to large rather flat double flowers of a pure cold white with exquisite frail looking veined petals and a delicious and characteristic scent. The only fault of this rose is that it does sometimes get spoiled by bad weather. Another beauty is 'Conrad Ferdinand Meyer' (1899) with big rounded flowers of silvery pink, fully double, its late flowers of superb quality; then there is 'Belle Poitevine' with loosely petalled mallow pink blooms, showing creamy stamens, and perhaps most sumptuous of all the rugosas, the 'Roseraie de L'Hay' (named for the famous French rose garden with flowers as delicately shaped as the famous alba rose 'Celeste', but coloured an intense crimson purple, double but with cream stamens visible. 'Fimbriata (1891). blush, with edges frilled like a pink (also known as 'Phoebe's frilled Pink') has endearing little flowers, lacking the coarseness of the later Grootendorst frilled hybrids. This and 'Schneelicht', a lovely single forming a splendid rounded bush of pale green foliage starred with white, show the range of choice amongst but one section of the late Victorian shrub roses.

The 'Ayrshire' roses, both hardy and vigorous, were less choice in flower but covered their whippy long growths with branches of small sweet pom-pom flowers in June. And also there was the older and much loved 'Felicité et Perpetue' (1840)—a climber with a china elegance of leaf (dark, pointed and almost evergreen) and highly double snow white flowers from red tinted buds, each small and shapely and deliciously scented, in large lax clusters.

The climbers were not far behind in beauty and refinement of flower. In 1896 'Aglaia' came out, a pale yellow climbing rose of great beauty, and before the new century was

M

very old the deep pink variety of Rose sinica anemone 'Romona' appeared. But Rose sinica and the older climbing Teas and Noisettes (typical being the glorious 'Rêve d'Or' of 1860, with butter yellow buds, a great plant of which was the glory of Charles Kingsley's Rectory at Eversley) were slightly tender and needed a warm wall. Far more vigorous were the foreign wild introductions made at the end of the century such as 'Rosa Soulieana' (1896, from West China) with enormous canes, covered with grey leaves and flowers with ivory yellow buds opening white, each an inch wide, in enormous bunches, yellow prickles and orange hips and a glorious fruity fragrance. 'R. Soulieana', seen at its best today at the great National Trust garden at Kiftsgate in Gloucestershire, is a typical country-house garden flower, really only suitable where there is enough space to let it wander at will.

So many of the spectacular introductions of the plant hunters of late Victorian times were only suitable for large gardens. In many old Cornish gardens, camellias and rhododendrons the size of forest trees, bent over with age and the weight of their flowers, droning with bees, and in America the enormous, venerable magnolias of the swamp gardens of St Louis, show what a scale such plants can attain. But even amongst the rhododendrons there are some Victorians which preserve a characteristic period grace but are small in size. *Broughtonii aureum* and *Smithii aureum* for example—both azalea-rhododendron crosses, each with butter yellow flowers (*Smithii* the deeper in colour) in shapely large trusses with decorative deeply channelled evergreen foliage—make large bushes rather than trees and have a compact and tidy habit of growth. Amongst the short list of small rhododendrons given by Robinson in his *English Flower Garden*, however, there is one Victorian introduction of great beauty, 'ciliatum', with deep rose pink buds opening to full pink or flushed white bells with tobacco brown stamens on a spreading bush which grows only about 3 feet high but which may be as much as 5 feet across, with evergreen foliage and young leaves of a delicious lime green. 'Ciliatum' covered in flower (and it is most generous in flower), satiny and rich though its individual bells are, preserves a wild flower grace infinitely preferable to the overwhelming effect of the later hybrid rhododendrons.

Many of the Victorian hardy hybrids and first crosses from the wild, however, had a refinement which the grander twentieth-century introductions have lost. *Fastuosum flore pleno* of a peculiarly soft purple, with hose in hose flowers which go perfectly with creamy yellow azaleas, *Govenianum* (lavender) and *Bodartianum*, with pale pink buds opening to a white flower with spotted throat, have an elegance about them which the more spectacular modern plants lack. Victorian rhododendrons generally have soft and subtle colours, 'Old Port' (wine-red), 'Baron Schroder' (plum with yellow centre), 'Joseph Whitworth' (dark purple lake with black-spotted throat), are examples of the dark shades, whilst 'Prince Camille de Rohan' is a soft crimson, dark-eyed and with frilled flowers and 'Bianchii' is a particularly pure pink, the only true pink free from all suspicion of rankness, as Miss Jekyll noted in the nineties. *Bianchii* and *Multi maculatum* (which she called 'multum maculatum' and a modern expert[1] calls 'Tondelayo') were two of Miss Jekyll's favourite rhododendrons. Much as she admired 'the great bouncing beauties' she said 'this most refined and delicate class of beauty equally deserves faithful championship', and she described *Multi maculatum* as 'of a delicate milk white, generously spotted with a rosy scarlet of the loveliest quality' with 'leaves the longest and narrowest and darkest green I know, making the bush conspicuously handsome in winter'. There were other lovely whites too; 'The Bride' (F.C.C. 1871) pure white with green-spotted eye, and 'Chionides'—older still—with a small cup-shaped truss of ivory white with a primrose yellow centre.

[1] Michael Haworth Booth: *Effective Flowering Shrubs.*

The names of many of these rhododendrons have an aristocratic ring. 'Lady Clementine Mitford' in delicate peach, 'Lady Grey Egerton' in soft mauve, 'Lady Eleanor Cathcart' in pink, were all early Victorians. 'The Countess of Derby' (F.C.C. 1877) and the 'Duchess of Teck' (F.C.C. 1879) are examples of later fashions in pink, whilst the 'Duchess of York' (A.M. 1894) in salmon, with a green-spotted throat is typical of the novelty colours which fin de siécle taste found so much to its liking. With 'Pink Pearl'—so very frilly and pink—in 1897, the modern hybrid rhododendrons had really begun.

The hardy hybrid rhododendrons are amongst the best Victoriana for large gardens. Those hybrids with *catawbiense* or *ponticum* blood are amongst the hardiest of shrubs, hardy enough for planting in New World gardens. But for smaller gardens the best hunting ground for Victoriana is found amongst the herbaceous plants.

The earliest decades are best represented by the florists' flowers: formal odd coloured but evenly marked show auriculas, show pansies, laced polyanthus, pinks, pelargoniums. Unfortunately few of the old names survive—although it is possible to buy seeds of strains raised from them—such as the 'Laced Polyanthus'. Many of the old pelargoniums, however, do exist: *L'Elegante* (1868), ivy leaved, with white leaf margins and delicate white flowers, feathered purple, *Black Vesuvius*—stout limbed and short, pale pink against almost beetroot dark leaves; crisp curled leaved aromatic pelargoniums—peppermint, lemon or 'Prince of Orange'—mauve flowered and orange scented or the celebrated 'Black Prince', most velvety of regals, with its blackish maroon shadings and fresh saw-toothed leaves. Most of these early types of pelargonium are available, also the ubiquitous bedding geraniums, including the insipid pink, ivy-leaved trailers, beloved of many of the late Victorians, but denounced by William Robinson.

Robinson's herbaceous flowers (those selected by Miss Jekyll) are worth seeking. Many of the plants they recommended have long been superseded by more showy modern varieties, however, for sheer garden quality rather than novelty and brightness of colour, they are worth finding. Perennial aster 'Climax' with its great branched stems of pure Wedgwood blue and clean golden centres is one. Another worthwhile Michaelmas daisy is 'Ericoides', with tiny white flowers; it produces a foam of white tiny flowers, almost like a gypsophila, perfect in its cobwebby elegance and grey white as a foil to rich autumn colour. Another white flower with a definite grace of its own is the white everlasting pea, used in flower arrangements with eryngium, the silvery blue sea holly, by Miss Jekyll. Miss Jekyll loved grey-leaved plants and one of her favourites, also recommended by William Robinson, is *Iris Pallida Dalmatica* 'clear pale bluish lavender lilac, 4 or 5 feet high, very prolific in flower with grey swords of foliage lasting in beauty all the year'.[1]

Both Robinson and Miss Jekyll were keen on the shape and colour of leaves. So one finds William Robinson appreciating the rich and varied colours of the young leaves of the newly introduced moutans or tree peonies (varieties he recommended, such as 'Elizabeth'—glowing salmon pink, double —and *Fiagrans maxima plena*—large fragrant pale pink—are still available today), the good form and growth of the older herbaceous types and the shape of such plants as the funkias (now hostas) with their great channelled glaucous leaves and lily-like flowers and verbasceums, specially phlomoides and olympicum—rising in spires of close packed yellow flowers above great felted rosettes of leaves.

Not all the flowers of the Robinson school of gardening were pale and silvery in colour, however. Lobelia cardinalis 'Huntsman' and 'Queen Victoria' were two plants of a really glowing scarlet which he commended. Both with decorative beetroot coloured foliage and fringed lobelia flowers (like the annual lobelia on a large scale) can be obtained today and in

[1] Graham Stuart Thomas: *A Modern Florilegium.*

a favourable season, in a rich peaty soil can be the glory of the garden.

The garden craft of William Robinson and Miss Jekyll produced gardens more beautiful in colour and texture than any since the great eighteenth-century landscape gardeners. They had the floral resources of nearly a century to use as material—cottage bred florist flowers, exotic shrubs brought home by plant collectors from abroad, roses in variety. They chose with restraint, Miss Jekyll planting for form and colour effects like an Impressionist painter (she had received a painter's training in colour). Her books on gardening, among them *Wood and Garden*, *Home and Garden* and *Colour in the Garden* (actually published 1907), are the best kind of Victoriana, timeless in the excellence of their taste and good sense.

INDEX